A SUCCESSION BLUEPRINT

The companion guide to *Four Voices*

JOHN VAMOS

Praise for *Four Voices*

'This book is a must-read for anyone involved in or interested in the dynamics of a family business. John clearly explains the terrain of what can be a very confusing and emotional situation and outlines how good governance can make it all straightforward. I highly recommend it.'

Darlene S Mayer, Mayer Family

'*Four Voices* shows an acute understanding of the complexities that lie within a multigenerational family business and offers reasonable and practical solutions to creating a foolproof succession plan. John is the Yoda of family business!'

Samuel J Lentini, CEO Eastcoast Beverages

'*Four Voices* by John Vamos has really changed the way I think about intergenerational wealth. After reading this book I was inspired to change some of our structure in order to separate some of the influences between family and business, wealth and governance to set ourselves up for success as we begin the transfer of wealth between generations. This book is a must-read for anyone wanting to set up their kids for success.'

Luke Geelan, CEO Geelan Property Group

'*Four Voices* is a fantastic summary of the complexity facing family business here in Australia regarding governance, succession and intergenerational wealth transfer. Navigating the complexities and emotional roller coaster is difficult for all families in business and for those that surround them – including family members, the business team members and the trusted external advisors. *Four Voices* and its author, John, provides clever frameworks to practically apply to assist and guide these families to a commercial and personal outcome. A very worthwhile read for all family business advisors and families in business. Highly recommended.'

Scott Young, Managing Partner, Altus Advisory

'John's knowledge of the human mind and our hard-wired behaviours, both at work and at home, is very enlightening and beneficial. It resonated for me not just in the business of managing succession, but in the everyday living. I recommend John's 'guide book' highly. Our family members and my six sons have all benefitted from reading *Four Voices*.'

Ross Colosimo, Founder of Momento Hospitality

'*Four Voices* provides us with a calm, methodical and practical approach to successfully navigating the ins and outs of family and complexity when significant family enterprise is involved. The book is supported with case studies and anecdotes that bring the issues to life – John's experience working for decades with clients is evident throughout.'

Alan Duncan, Founder, Private Wealth Network

'John has written a very practical guide to a facilitation of wealth transfer through generations. The book recognises that each family will face challenges that are unique to that family but can apply a collaborative framework to optimise outcomes for each individual family member, and the family as a whole. John understands that the subject of succession planning is uncomfortable for many people and the book acknowledges that non-financial legacies are also important. *Four Voices* is a great guide for any advisor looking to add value to a long-term relationship with any family group.'

Geoff Stein, Partner, Brown Wright Stein

'There is no question that following John's advice will create a better business and family life!'

Steve Vamos, Author and former CEO Xero Limited

First published in 2025 by John Vamos

© John Vamos 2025
The moral rights of the author have been asserted

All rights reserved. Except as permitted under the *Australian Copyright Act 1968* (for example, a fair dealing for the purposes of study, research, criticism or review), no part of this book may be reproduced, stored in a retrieval system, communicated or transmitted in any form or by any means without prior written permission. No part of this book may be used or reproduced in any manner for the purpose of training artificial intelligence technologies or systems.

All inquiries should be made to the author.

A catalogue entry for this book is available from the National Library of Australia.

Book production and text design by Publish Central
Cover design by Pipeline Design

The paper this book is printed on is certified as environmentally friendly.

Disclaimer: The material in this publication is of the nature of general comment only, and does not represent professional advice. It is not intended to provide specific guidance for particular circumstances and it should not be relied on as the basis for any decision to take action or not take action on any matter which it covers. Readers should obtain professional advice where appropriate before making any such decision. To the maximum extent permitted by law, the author and publisher disclaim all responsibility and liability to any person, arising directly or indirectly from any person taking or not taking action based on the information in this publication.

Contents

About the Author	1
Introduction	3
Cast of Characters	7
First Meeting: Background	15
Second Meeting: Current Reality	31
Third Meeting: Understanding Happiness	47
Fourth (and Final) Meeting: The Solution	69
Epilogue	95
Endnotes	101

About the Author

John Vamos has worked alongside businesses for over 35 years, including many of Australia's most successful, wealthy and enduring family dynasties. Regarded by many as the father of business coaching in Australia, John was certainly the first to apply 'business coaching' as a professional designation. Over three decades he has also been the lead strategic facilitator for many of Australia's top 200 public and private companies.

A law graduate with 15 years of financial advisory experience, overlapping 35 years as a business coach, John has witnessed first-hand the unique and especially complex issues that face family enterprises. He has met countless struggling business leaders inside family enterprises who are confused by the reality they find themselves in – everything from succession issues to business dysfunction to sibling rivalry to family disunity and fracture.

The creator of the highly successful Thinking System suite of tools, John uses these tried-and-tested techniques to address these and other thorny family business issues. The Thinking System can liberate any type of business from any type of challenge, but the rewards of resolution can be especially miraculous in family business.

John is the author of four books. The first, *You Don't Think as Smart as You Are*, explored how being human challenges productivity. The second, *Elephants and the Business Laws of Nature*, looked more closely at these issues in the context of business management. The third, *Four Voices* – John's magnum opus – is dedicated to unravelling how those same human issues not only play out in family enterprise, but are amplified by family enterprise! This book, *A Succession Blueprint*, is a companion guide to *Four Voices*. It is a whistlestop tour of those issues inside an imaginary family: the Jacksons. It outlines exactly what can be done to mitigate and nullify these universal problems, so that each family business can successfully defend love, loyalty, family wealth, and succession through the generations.

https://fourvoicesadvisory.com.au/

Introduction

When it comes to family wealth there is a curse active throughout the world. Namely, that the first generation (G1) makes it, the second generation (G2) enjoys it and the third generation (G3) destroys it! Rags to riches and back again in three generations.

Of course, the curse is not inevitable – G2 and G3 may be as successful as, or even more successful than, the founder. When we investigate those who *are*, we discover that their success is always aided and abetted by G1's positive actions. And these actions are far easier to accomplish successfully in the hands of the founding generation (G1).

The issue that prevents G1 from taking these actions is that, too often, the generation that seeds the wealth (G1) thinks the critical rules and lessons learnt in the making of the money are the same as the knowledge needed for the defence of the money. And yet, the management of an enduring multigenerational family business and the governance of wealth is a completely different science to the science of entrepreneurship and making the money in the first place. While each generation must learn the ropes of their respective industry or business, there are very few lessons to be learnt about the starting of that business that are necessary or applicable to family governance, succession, or continued growth. The inventor or founder of a business is rarely going to successfully transition that business to the next generation and beyond by teaching those individuals how they invented a product or started that business. The information and knowledge needed to develop a business, take it forward and maintain and develop wealth for each successive generation are *very* different from the entrepreneurial mindset so often present in founders.

American scholar HL Mencken said, 'For every complex problem there is an answer that is clear, simple, and wrong.' The assumption that a wealth creator is motivated to see their heirs replicate or exceed their accomplishments is clear, simple and wrong. Family with multigenerational wealth is a *very* complex problem. Assuming that it will somehow work itself out because 'we're family' and 'blood is thicker than water' is also clear, simple and wrong.

If G1 is serious about succession and wants to create an enduring legacy, they need to stop lamenting that G2 are unworthy, often actively taking steps to ensure they remain unworthy. Instead, G1 must master stewardship, putting things in place that will allow G2 (and beyond) *to be worthy and ready* for succession.

If G2 is serious about being worthy and ready, they must accept that they can't inherit their father's or mother's job just because they have the same surname! G2 can inherit shares, rights and influence but they can't inherit a job – they can only earn it. This fact is blindingly obvious in all areas of life – except family business. If one of your parents is an eye surgeon and they die suddenly, you don't expect a phone call from the hospital to say you are now their go-to eye surgeon and you are expected in theatre in two hours. The idea is ludicrous, and yet it is expected and almost inevitable in a family business.

If the family business curse is true, and the statistics confirm that it is, then this rags-to-riches boomerang represents a colossal waste. Not just the staggering loss of the accumulated wealth of the family business but the human cost too – the people who are no longer employed by these businesses, the communities they no longer serve and the breakdown of family connection, love and loyalty that the curse facilitates.

But it doesn't have to be this way.

Managing love, loyalty and family wealth successfully generation after generation comes down to your willingness and determination to allow four distinct voices to be heard:

1. The business (or balance sheet).
2. The individuals (founder and family members).
3. The family (collectively).
4. The family community (spouses and future generations).

I wrote *Four Voices: Managing love, loyalty, family wealth and succession through the generations* as a full explanation of why family business is so challenging and what to do about it. But you are busy – I get it. It's a big book!

Those who read it loved it, and they particularly enjoyed reading about the Jacksons – a fictional family whose stories I shared to help illustrate the challenges in family business and how they can so easily create a Gordian Knot of complexity, hostility and angst. Readers loved the Jacksons because they recognised the family members and their issues in their own family dynamic.

This companion guide, therefore, focuses on the conversation between co-founders John and Ayesha Jackson and their trusted advisor, during a series of meetings where they are desperate to better understand the challenges they face and find a proven solution. My hope is that by the end of this much shorter book, you will be suitably inspired to read *Four Voices* – the source code for elegant succession in families of enterprise and wealth.

Cast of Characters

John is an Australian migrant, having arrived from England when he was five years old. Making Australia his home, John got into construction straight out of school and started Jackson Developments & Construction with his wife, Ayesha, in 1983.

Over the years, the business has become very successful. John and Ayesha could easily sell and live a life of luxury, but the business is their first child and John, especially, is still very attached to it. He loves the challenge and enjoys the hard work. He wants to stick around and dabble, and more than anything, he wants to leave a legacy. Typical of first generations (G1s) with children, John can't make up his mind which, if any, of his children should take over the business. If he's honest, he's not sure any of them are up to the task. Each have their own strengths (and weaknesses), but none seem to have his all-around experience or insight.

John is stuck. He wants to step back but doesn't know how or when to do so, and he's not comfortable making that lifestyle change until he feels confident the business is in good hands. But he genuinely doesn't know whose hands are safe hands, and is reluctant to make a decision because he knows that whatever decision he makes will cause problems within the family.

**Ayesha** is also a migrant, arriving from Sri Lanka as a child in the mid-1960s. Like John's parents, Ayesha's carved out a life and a home in Australia through sheer hard work and determination. Australia has always been home for both Ayesha and John.

Ayesha and John were married when she was 20 and he was 24. Christopher was born in 1985. Priya followed a year later, then Nathan and Anika. Ayesha continued to work with John after Christopher was born, but stopped once Priya arrived. John had moved from renovations and subdivisions to building and property development. When the children were in school, Ayesha went back to work for the business and stayed involved for many years.

Ayesha can see John's hesitation around succession. He's old school so doesn't really believe that Priya, as a woman, can manage the business. Ayesha works hard to dispel that myth but she's not convinced she's making any headway. She knows he recognises parts of each of his sons' natures as positive for the business, but those positive parts are not in the same son! Nathan has his qualities and his drawbacks, as does Christopher, so there is no logical or clear choice to step into his leadership role.

Ayesha has always worried about Christopher and Nathan as they have never seen eye to eye or been friends. They love each other but don't necessarily like each other, and she can't see how that would work in a business where one would need to be in charge.

Ayesha is stuck because she can see what the situation is doing to John *and* their children.

Christopher, as the oldest son, has always felt the burden of succession, even though he is also acutely aware that his dad isn't convinced he's the right man for the job. Christopher is sure he would have preferred that Nathan be the eldest son. Nathan is much more like John in looks and temperament. But John is traditional, so the idea that the eldest son should succeed him still holds sway. Christopher and John are, however, very different people. John is a hands-on, shorts and work boots kind of guy. He built the business up from nothing and did everything in the business, onsite and off. Christopher is a back-office thinker. He's always been happier working in a T-shirt and jeans on the creative side of the business rather than onsite, knee deep in mud. This is why he studied architecture. If he was being honest with himself, he would probably have preferred graphic design but he decided that architecture was a good compromise that might keep his dad happy. He's not sure it has.

In many ways, Christopher is trying to find his own path while staying involved in the family business. He loves John and doesn't want to disappoint him, but he dislikes Nathan and has zero interest in working under him or over him. Although he often feels diminished by John and Nathan's relationship, as though they are both in on some private joke he doesn't understand, he does enjoy being involved in the family business. He's just not sure he wants to get involved in all the parts of the business, which being CEO would demand.

Christopher is stuck living a half-life, trying to keep his father happy but keep himself and his own growing family happy too.

A SUCCESSION BLUEPRINT

CAST OF CHARACTERS

Priya is the smartest of the four children, at least academically. Certainly, smarter than Nathan, who appears to be the one most likely to take over the family firm. Priya is closer to Christopher and can see how he struggles to find his place.

She has the same struggle. Despite proving herself repeatedly in the business, and gaining a masters in engineering, she is still seen first and foremost as the boss's daughter. Not *child* but *daughter*. She's irritated that her salary is nowhere near what her brothers make, despite being more qualified than both of them and doing equally important work.

Like Christopher, she has limited interest in working in the business if Nathan takes over, and as much as she believes he has talents and is a valuable asset to the business, she doesn't feel he has the nuance or brains to run it. Priya is thinking it may be time to leave.

Priya is also stuck because she can't get her dad to take her seriously, and if she leaves the business, she's worried she might never get back in.

Nathan worked his way up in the business from school. He's had experience in most departments and understands the processes of building very well. As such, he believes (although he doesn't voice his belief) that he does most of the work and has, for all intents and purposes, taken over the top job from his dad.

In personality, looks and nature, Nathan is most like John, and he knows it. Nathan uses the difference between John and Christopher to stir up trouble and mock Christopher at pretty much every opportunity. He is also savvy enough to work that similarity with John in his favour – hence his belief that he will get the top job. He believes that

John connects with him in a way he doesn't with his other children, largely because John worked his way up in the building industry too. But this isn't true; John is proud of all his kids for different reasons. But it doesn't stop Nathan believing and acting as though he is the favourite.

Nathan is also angry about his salary. His irritation stems from the fact that both he and Christopher earn the same but Christopher, who is a qualified architect, only works part-time in the family business. He has his own architectural firm, too. Nathan is sure that a good architect could be found for half the price. He's been told many times that Christopher bills the family business at a significant discount, but he doesn't believe it.

Nathan is also stuck because he doesn't have any qualifications to fall back on, unlike his siblings. He's not ready to set up on his own, so his only options would be to work for a competitor and that doesn't feel right. He's also stuck because he believes he's entitled to take over the business now. Why should it matter who was born first?

Anika never really paid that much attention to the family business. As the youngest there were already too many siblings vying for attention in that regard. She knew pretty early on that she needed to forge her own path outside the business. But she is aware of the family wealth after something was said in passing at a Christmas gathering that made her realise the extent of that wealth. Now she is worried that her lack of attention will prevent her and her own family from benefiting from it. And to make matters worse, she feels intense guilt for having those thoughts. She has recently opened her own restaurant, The Surf Shack, with the help of her parents but it has already caused friction in her relationship with her brothers and sister.

Anika is stuck too because she is as much part of the family as her siblings; and yet, if she benefits in any way from the wealth the business has created, she is made to feel guilty. She is also a mum and is concerned that her own children will miss out on a better life because she didn't get involved in the family business. Anika also knows, having watched Priya struggle, that another daughter in the business would not have been considered that useful by her dad. Her heart tells her this is ridiculous, and she pursued a meaningful career, but her head is telling her that, financially at least, she may have made a huge mistake.

First Meeting: Background

When a family shares their story, it is important for the advisor not only to listen to the words they say, but also to listen for clues about the founder profile, the next generation profile, the family dynamics and the trusted advisor framework. In other words, the answers to just four questions:

1. **Is the founder motivated to find a solution?**
   - ☐ Yes
   - ☐ No

2. **Is the next generation ready?**
   - ☐ Ready and impatient
   - ☐ Ready and patient
   - ☐ Not ready

3. **What is the level of family hostility or dysfunction?**
   - ☐ Normal levels of family dysfunction
   - ☐ Open hostility and angst

4. **Does the family have a history of employing trusted advisors when needed?**
   - ☐ Yes
   - ☐ No

In terms of the above questions, John is motivated, albeit a little reluctant to fully step away. The next generation are ready and impatient but are unclear of their roles or career progression and opportunities. The level of family dysfunction is mainly normal, but there are moments of hostility and above-average levels of angst. On the bright side, they can all be in the same room as each other without the prospect of violence. There is, however, an unspoken undercurrent within the family that the status quo is about to change depending on what John decides about succession. As for trusted advisors, the family is used to employing them from time to time, although they are more familiar with employing a lawyer or accountant rather than a governance advisor.

Overall, the Jackson family business is functional and successful. But it's largely ungoverned. There is no formal governance. John is the walking, talking governance system in that what he says – goes. This means that everything will probably tick along well until John dies or becomes seriously ill. If there is no governance in place before that happens then chaos and dysfunction are almost inevitable.

Thankfully, John and Ayesha are smart enough to recognise that they need some help and some much-needed objectivity. Every family business is woefully short on objectivity. So, they decide to take the bull by the horns and ask their trusted governance advisor to meet with them. Both founders recognise the challenges on the horizon. In truth, many of those challenges are in the here and now.

John opened the first meeting by saying, 'Thanks for making the time to see us. It's probably long overdue, but before we begin, we just want to flag what's important to us. We are not interested in being bamboozled with industry jargon or any fancy theory that some academic thinks might work. What we are after is a proven business process or blueprint that the whole family can get behind, so we can find solutions and stay connected as a family. I love my business, but I love our family more, and I know Ayesha feels the same. So, is there a way for us all to become unstuck?'

'There is,' said the trusted advisor. 'What I suggest is a very short agenda where you tell me about the business and the challenges you are facing, I explain the root cause of some of those issues and together we will map a path forward. How does that sound?'

'That sounds perfect,' replied John.

'Okay, let's start by you giving me a little bit of background on each of you. John, you go first. What's your story?'

'I arrived in Australia from England with my parents and two brothers when I was five years old. I don't remember England, and we never went back. It was too far away and too expensive. My relationship with my brothers was typical – friendly one minute, knocking seven bells out of each other the next – a bit like Christopher and Nathan. Although their sparring is more verbal than physical.

'My parents were strict and uncompromising – they had to be. Arriving in a new country with three children, our only advantage was that we spoke the language. Dad worked long hours in a warehouse – we didn't see him much. Mum stayed at home but worked a part-time job in the evenings once dad came home. I remember being conscious of how hard they worked and was determined to create a better life for my family.

'My first job out of school was in construction and I bought my first property in the inner west of Sydney when I was just 22.'

'That's impressive,' said the advisor.

John laughed, 'You wouldn't say that if you saw it – it was definitely a fixer-upper. It was also a very steep and expensive learning curve, but I enjoyed the process and wondered if there was scope for more.'

Ayesha continued, 'John and I had met around the time he bought that first property and we got married not long after. John was 24 and I was just 20 years old! Like John, I wasn't born in Australia. My parents were from Sri Lanka, arriving in Australia in the mid-1960s. They worked hard to make a life here, just like John's family, and both of us have always called Australia home.'

Looking at his wife, John reminisced, 'We were happy. We bought another property together as the family home and set about renovating it. Coming from different backgrounds was a source of amusement for both of us as we bumped up against different ideas, customs and value systems. But it was harder once we had kids.'

'This is common,' said the advisor. 'What's fascinating about families is that different value systems are often a source of endearment and attraction when two people meet; but as soon as children come along, those same endearing differences can easily become a source of tension, as both parents seek to raise their children from within their own value system and belief structure. The way we see the world is coloured by our own upbringing in a process called conditioning, which I'll come back to. By the time we reach adulthood we have formed quite rigid ideas of what is right and wrong – including how best to raise children. If our upbringing was good, we will strive to replicate it, and if it wasn't good we will deliberately deviate from it – wanting something better for our own children. In other words, we adjust how we raise our children based on what we think worked from our own upbringing, *and* what we think didn't work. In large part, we believe our upbringing was the "right way" – even if we recognise that it was flawed. Or we believe our upbringing was the "wrong way" and rail against it. Either way, it is rare for two parents from two different backgrounds and cultures with different value systems to agree on how best to raise their children.'

'I never thought of it like that,' said Ayesha. 'But that makes sense, and it was certainly true for us.'

John nodded, 'It was, I can still remember us bickering about silly little things around what was best for the kids. And those things were probably because of my English heritage and your Sri Lankan heritage.'

'Exactly!' said the advisor.

'Looking back, though,' added John, 'I think our first "child" was Jackson Developments & Construction. Our first project was a house on a large block of land in Maroubra, New South Wales, which we demolished, building a duplex in its place.'

John turned to Ayesha, 'Remember how nerve-wracking that was!'

'Yes,' she replied. 'But it was also exhilarating when it all came together.'

'Things certainly got more complicated when our other kids came along,' added John. 'Christopher was born in 1985 and that was amazing and scary at the same time! There is no handbook for parenting and we felt like we were just making it up as we went along.'

Ayesha continued, 'Priya followed a year later, then Nathan and Anika. I continued to work after Christopher was born, but it became impossible once Priya arrived. But the business was doing well. Initially John focused on subdividing large garden blocks and building another house, or flattening the existing house and creating a duplex or small block of apartments. Sydney was booming so business was thriving. Once the children were all at school, I came back to work in the business doing the books, scheduling tradesmen, and organising deliveries to the various sites.'

'Raising four children alongside her work in the business helped her develop expert negotiation and organisational skills,' added John. 'She would drop the children at school and go on to the office. If any of the children were sick, the school nurse would put them in a taxi, they would arrive at the office and Ayesha would tuck them up in the break room with a blanket, a mug of steaming hot tomato soup, some toast, and the remote control for the TV. If it was more than a sniffle she would take them home along with a pile of folders. I would never have managed without her.'

'So were all the children aware of the business as they were growing up, or did you keep it separate?' asked the advisor.

'They were all aware – it was all we ever talked about really,' John continued. 'Or certainly it was all the kids ever heard us talking about! Having a family business, especially in the early years, is consuming. It's impossible to separate the business from the family – everything just merges together, and whenever the family were together, it was always being discussed around the table along with what had happened at school or following up on homework.

'As they got older, the boys were expected to work on the various building sites,' added Ayesha. 'I was always nagging him to take Priya too because she was just as interested and I could see she was feeling ignored by her dad.'

'I just noticed you rolling your eyes there, John,' said the advisor. 'Would you like to elaborate?'

'This has been one of those endless conversations between us. I adore Priya, Ayesha knows that, and I knew she wanted to come with me, but I just couldn't see the point. There were no women running construction businesses back then, and even now there are very few. Priya was strong enough and enjoyed sport when she was young but that's a world away from the bullshit that happens on building sites. I didn't want her anywhere near that. It may be old-fashioned and it may even be sexist but I'm never going to change my mind on that. A building site is no place for a girl, even now! And yes before you ask, I did secretly wish that it was Christopher or Nathan who showed as much interest.'

'How did Priya respond to that?' asked the advisor.

'She never knew – it's not like I told her that!' John replied defensively.

'Don't be ridiculous, John. You may have thought your thoughts were your own but Priya knew! As far as she was concerned your indifference oozed from every pore. She knew you loved her but you frequently dismissed her because she was a girl. Even when Priya challenged your attitude, you would fob her off by saying you were just joking or it was just banter. I think her defensiveness, especially when she got angry, just confirmed your opinion that she didn't belong in the construction world.'

'Well, it's true!' muttered John. 'It certainly was then. I get that a lot has changed but it was rough when I started!'

'If I may, I'd like to jump in here just to explain a little about that situation,' said the advisor. 'When faced with challenges, it's very easy to look outside for answers, but the source of a lot of the problems we face in all walks of life is actually in the other direction – we need to look inwards.'

'What do you mean?' chimed John and Ayesha in unison.

'I won't go into too much detail at this point but human beings are not born ready. A baby antelope or bison is running alongside its mother within minutes of birth. A baby tortoise hatches from an egg, digs itself out of the sand and scuttles to the ocean by moonlight without any parental supervision whatsoever. But a human baby is utterly useless for the first few years of their life (for some it can be much longer!).'

'Ain't that the truth,' laughed John.

The advisor continued, 'Human beings get ready through associative conditioning – the process I mentioned earlier. This is often called Hebb's Law – "what fires together wires together."[1] In 1949, Donald Hebb, a Canadian neuropsychologist, presented a theory of learning suggesting we learn new information when our brain forms new synaptic connections – increasing our capacity to remember by forming associations between the known and the unknown. This is why metaphor and analogy work so well as a communication tool – they compare something that is known to something that is unknown, narrowing the comprehension gap.

'What we believe about the world – what is "right", "wrong", "acceptable", "unacceptable", "possible", "impossible", "good" or "bad" – is learned through this conditioning process. John's attitude to Priya and her suitability to be in the family business, never mind lead it, is not a conscious choice, although he will be able to come up with all sorts of logical reasons to justify that thinking. But the source of that belief is not rational, it's been conditioned into him by his upbringing.

'John, when you were young, did you ever see women in leadership roles?' asked the advisor.

'Well, no, mum was at home looking after us, she did work but I never saw her at work. And it was the same with family friends. All I ever experienced was women in the home.'

'Exactly! That's my point,' added the advisor. 'You never witnessed women working much outside the home or in a corporate setting. As a result, you were conditioned to believe that women didn't really work outside the home. And this holds true for you even though women's potential is evident throughout society and across every culture, from science to business to politics and beyond. Your beliefs, not just about women in the workplace but about pretty much everything else, are conditioned responses that become your default settings.'

'Okay, but that doesn't make them wrong,' added John.

'True. But it doesn't make them right either. Renowned physician Gabor Maté emphasises that our unconscious attitudes profoundly shape our children's emotional and psychological development. He argues that children are highly attuned to the emotional states and inner worlds of their parents or primary caregivers, even those emotions and beliefs they don't express directly. According to Maté, these internal states can be "transmitted" to children through subtle nonverbal cues such as body language, tone of voice, or patterns of attention and absence. Even if a parent is doing everything "right" on the surface, being attentive, providing for their child, setting rules, their unconscious stress or emotional wounds can create a disconnect that the child feels but doesn't understand.[2] The unintended consequences of your beliefs around women on building sites are Priya's feelings of closed doors and denied opportunities. That's just a developmental fact.

'We can't reach adulthood without these default settings. It's impossible. And they are designed to make life easier and safer. They become reflex responses that automate our decision making and shortcut thinking. In fact, when a default has been activated, we are not "thinking" at all. It's the cognitive equivalent of a doctor tapping your knee with a little rubber hammer to test your reflexes. Your knee kicks out – but "you" didn't do it. It's an automatic response to the rubber hammer, and default settings do the same via reflex responses.

'Think of these brain default settings like the default settings on your computer. When you buy a new computer, you remove it from its box and plug it in – it's ready to go. The software and the hardware are already configured to do what most users would want to do with that type of computer, whether that's prepare documents or play graphics-heavy games. It's safer and easier that way. Safer because the manufacturer's help line won't be clogged up with people asking stupid questions, and easier for the customer to get the most out of their new machine. If we bought a new computer and we had to load all the software and fiddle around with the settings, most of us would lose the will to live. So, all that is taken care of for us. We can change the settings, but most users never do. Most of us have absolutely no idea the extent of the additional functionality that even a mid-range computer could deliver if we changed the default settings the machine comes with. And the same is true with the brain. Its default settings are developed over time because of conditioning and they create reflex responses.

'These default settings, also known as prejudices or biases, blind you to any alternative reality. But don't worry; we all have thousands of these default settings that tell us what is right, wrong, acceptable, unacceptable, good, bad, possible and impossible. And these conditioned stereotypes are, of course, reinforced by the nature of your business, which you believe to be hard, physically demanding, male-dominated work.

'Does that sound plausible to you?' asked the advisor.

'Well, yes … I guess so,' admitted John.

'But the brawn that was required to be successful in your profession when you started has largely been replaced by machinery that anyone can operate. It's brains, male or female, that are now the most important ingredient for your business's success. Is that not also true?'

'I suppose so,' said John, 'but men can be very crude on a building site, and I just don't want Priya to be around that!'

Ayesha jumped in: 'I know John, but we have not raised a mouse! Priya is a strong young woman, more than capable of giving as good as she gets, and people would come to accept that.'

'The point I am trying to make here,' added the advisor, 'is that conditioning is an automatic learning mechanism born out of biological imperative – the drive to survive. It kicks in almost as soon as we are born and long before we can speak. John, you were never consciously taught your conditioned beliefs about gender; you simply picked them up from the environment you grew up in. And that is true for you too, Ayesha. It's true for all of us, and we are going through life believing that we are making rational choices when what we are really doing is a knee-jerk reaction to long-forgotten events and situations that occurred on the way to "ready".'

'But I worked in the business,' said Ayesha. 'So that doesn't make sense.'

'It does actually love, you worked in the office and I only agreed to you helping when the kids were at school because I really needed someone I could trust and I didn't really want to add another salary to the payroll!' admitted John rather sheepishly.

'But you absolutely proved me wrong,' said John, looking for redemption. 'You were invaluable, but I suppose my cultural upbringing still limited my opinion of how our daughters might be involved. And if we are being super honest here – even though Priya did engineering, I've always been a bit scared that she would just get married, have children and leave!'

'Oh, for heaven's sake John – it's not the 1800s you know,' admonished Ayesha.

'Anyway,' said the advisor, 'it's just important to recognise that the beliefs we have may not be valid or accurate and they may require more conscious enquiry to determine if they are useful or not. But let's move on for now … Tell me about your children.'

'To tell you the truth,' said John, 'Chris confuses me. For a start, he hates being called Chris and insists on Christopher. We are nothing like each other. As a child, he wasn't sporty and would avoid being outside if he could help it. He preferred drawing or coming up with ideas for short animated films. Nathan was more like me, and he would follow me around when he was little. I'd put him in the ute on a Saturday morning and the two of us would go and visit various work sites or drive around a suburb looking for potential development sites.'

'Anika's not really that interested in the family business,' added Ayesha. 'She always wanted to be a chef. By the time John and Nathan arrived home she would have prepared a family lunch for everyone. Priya would arrive home from hockey and Christopher would emerge from his room – enticed out by the smell of something tasty from the kitchen.'

'So who is the most academic?' asked the advisor.

Both responded in unison, 'Priya'. Ayesha added, 'She's certainly smarter than Nathan. Christopher is also very bright, but his ability leans toward the creative. He was much more interested in how something looked than how it was built. And Anika has good business smarts. I keep reminding John to try and see each of our children for their unique gifts, but I think he finds it hard because there isn't a clear "winner" in terms of succession. Nathan is certainly more like John and that could be useful; but Christopher's skillset is also very important for the business moving forward. And there is certainly no reason in the modern world where machines do the hard work that either of the girls couldn't run a property development business.'

'That's about right,' added John, 'although even if I accept that a woman can run a construction business, Anika is happy with her chosen career and is happy in her restaurant.'

'That makes sense,' replied the advisor. 'So, what are the current expectations around the business with your other three children?'

'Nathan thinks he should get my job,' said John, 'but all the weight of expectation regarding the business is probably heaped on the shoulders of Christopher as our first-born son.'

'Again,' added the advisor, 'this is a conditioning thing. It's just a cultural expectation that first-born children, especially first-born sons, take over businesses. Certainly, there are countries around the world that still operate on this basis, it's still accepted and it still "works" to some extent. But we live in Australia, and as Ayesha rightly pointed out, we are not in the 1800s any more! Machinery and technological advances mean that brains are more important than brawn in most industries.'

'True,' pondered John. 'Christopher certainly still feels the weight of that expectation but he's not really that interested in the business. That is, in turn, creating a huge amount of resentment from Nathan and Priya who *are* interested in taking the business forward. Christopher and Nathan never really got on. They were reasonably friendly when they were young – although Nathan, who was physically bigger, often bullied Christopher. Once the testosterone kicked in it got worse and the "alpha male" competition started as they jostled for position. They were constantly fighting during their teenage years.'

'Yes, but it never bothered you,' added Ayesha. 'I think you just felt it was normal "boys being boys" stuff. You fought with your brothers all the time at their age. It demonstrated aggression and fighting spirit – both of which you believe are necessary for success in business.'

'Yeah,' admitted John. 'But I'm not bloody loving it much now because they are all turning their aggression or simmering hostility towards me! Nathan especially is trying to throw his weight around in the business, and it's not on. I just don't understand why it's become so gnarly ... I've always encouraged them to pursue their dreams and made it clear they could do whatever they wanted.'

'Really?! You can't seriously believe that, John,' said Ayesha. 'Sure, there may not have been any ultimatums or screaming matches, but the boys were under no illusion that they were expected to join the business and that one of them would take over when you decided to step down. The girls could do something in the business if they *really* wanted to, maybe HR or business development, but their role was never going to be CEO. You made that very clear from a very early age.'

'Well, if it makes you feel any better,' said the advisor, 'almost every founder of a family business I've ever met had those same expectations – conscious or not. It's just human nature to want to build the business, and family members almost always get involved in that process, especially in the early years. And the assumption is that involvement continues in some form or another.

'Okay,' added the advisor, 'I think this is a great place to stop for the day. To recap, you are both looking to step away from the business, or at least step back and, naturally, you want one of your kids to step into that CEO role. But although each has skills and experience that are helpful, each has their own drawbacks, so you don't know what to do to ensure a smooth transition that is good for you, your family and the wealth you have created.'

'Yes, that's basically it,' said John.

'Okay great, but what you also need to remember is you have created a very successful business and a lovely family. You should both be very proud. You are 63 John and you are 59 Ayesha – the next chapter awaits. And listen, every family business, especially the ones that have generated significant wealth, goes through what you are going through. And I promise, you are in a far better position than many founders or founder couples I meet. Often their children don't like each other and it's not even possible for them to be in the same room. By taking steps now, when things are not too corrupted by default settings and intense emotion, you can forge a solid path forward that works for you and all your children … Let's pick this up again tomorrow morning.'

Second Meeting: Current Reality

'Morning. I want to start this morning by unpacking where you and your children are in regard to the business,' suggests the advisor.

Ayesha kicks off: 'They are all doing their thing, including building families of their own. All are married with at least one child, except Priya who is engaged to her partner Delvyn. The problem is they are all confused about what's going to happen with the wealth the business has created and the business itself. Christopher is doing his best to appease his dad, but is conscious he's not really considered up to snuff. Nathan is irritated that he can't just be fast-tracked to John's 2IC. And Priya is angry that despite doing a master's in engineering she is still seen as junior to Nathan and Christopher. Anika has no interest in the business and is focused on her restaurant, The Surf Shack. We helped her to open it a few years back but even that caused all sorts of issues.'

'Tell me about that,' said the advisor.

John picked up the story: 'When Anika opened her restaurant, the whole family was invited to the opening. It was just a small place – 10 tables – but it was a start and she was over the moon. The evening was going reasonably well but there was a distinct undercurrent. Christopher especially seemed out of sorts. Nothing was said at the time and everyone did their best to enjoy the evening and support

Anika. For weeks afterwards, I noticed a few snipes towards Anika from Christopher and Nathan. Christopher muttered under his breath how nice it must be to be supported to follow your dreams – that sort of thing. Nathan made some comment about how there seems to be plenty of money for some people in the family but not others. After a few weeks, when the atmosphere hadn't lifted, I called everyone together to ask if there was anything that was upsetting them. Of course, no one admitted to anything but I wondered if they had jumped to conclusions about Anika's restaurant. You mentioned earlier about conditioning and how that creates default settings. Well our children have experienced quite different lives.'

'Of the four children,' added Ayesha, 'Christopher and Priya still remember their first home: a three-bedroom house in Glebe. Nathan and Anika only remember the six-bedroom house with manicured garden and pool in Bellevue Hill. Money was tight in Glebe and Christopher and Priya earned pocket money by working in the business after school and on weekends. Nathan would go with John on weekends, but he also played sport so he was given an allowance. By the time Anika came along, money was not an issue so she received an allowance without having to do any chores in exchange.'

'We are aware that Christopher and Priya think that we have spoilt the other two, especially Anika,' said John, 'So, I wondered if that was what was going on again. They thought Anika had just been given money. So I took a leap of faith and said I wanted to explain something. I felt that something had been brewing since Anika opened her restaurant. I apologised for not making it clearer before, but mum and I had invested 50 per cent of the restaurant start-up funding and Anika was paying that money back over the next 10 years at a bit less than her bank's interest rates.'

'It was like a cloud lifted,' added Ayesha. 'We couldn't believe it – you could feel the change in the room immediately. And John made it clear that the same offer extended to the other three should they have ideas or opportunities that required investment and support. All they would need to do was prepare a business and financial plan in the same way Anika had for her restaurant.'

'Priya spoke first,' said John. 'She said, "Really? Oh, right, we thought you had just given her the money … "'

'This goes back to those default settings,' said the advisor. 'One of the biggest default settings we have is that in the absence of information we will always default to the worst probable outcome. This is a survival thing again, and it makes sense. When we were hunter-gatherers, we didn't know if the red berries were poisonous so we defaulted to the worst probable outcome – they were – and chose not to eat them.

'In this situation, in the absence of information about how you supported Anika,' added the advisor, 'they all defaulted to the worst probable outcome, which was that, "She is spoilt and has always been spoilt." That, in turn, kicked off a raft of emotional reactions from irritation to anger and probably also guilt for being so petty.

'Research quite clearly shows,' continued the advisor, 'that emotional responses do not require facts or details prior to engagement. This means that we instinctively race to conclusions within milliseconds of any situation or event; we will unconsciously comprehend what it is, our minds then decide for us whether we like it or not, present that to our awareness as "fact" and happily form an opinion about it – all in a matter of seconds! Our emotions quite literally have a mind of their own, and that mind is not necessarily in sync with the mind we recognise as "I". We all know that it's best to get all the data and facts before we act. We are reminded not to jump to conclusions but, at least biologically, it's very difficult not to. Without the right information, Christopher, Nathan and Priya jumped to the conclusion that Anika had been gifted a lot of money for her restaurant. That assumption created emotional tension and animosity between the siblings and their parents – all unfounded and unnecessary. The associative learning and conditioning process means that our brain is always herding us towards a speedy predetermined conclusion such as "Typical! The baby gets spoilt again." Remember, these neurological realities are brain shortcuts. They allow us to arrive at a conclusion or decision so we can move on. But they pollute our thinking. And they are certainly not the result of the neocortex or superior cognitive process.'

Sitting down next to John and Ayesha for a moment, the advisor continued, 'The common denominator between family, business, wealth and the myriad challenges they generate is *people*. This is so obvious that we disregard its relevance, but to do so is a profound mistake. Most of the issues we face in life, family, business and beyond are down to our ignorance or dismissal of the human component. It's a component that is not unique to each family or to individual personalities, but common among our species. As Professor Nigel Nicholson once said, "You can take the person out of the Stone Age, but you can't take the Stone Age out of the person."[3]

'We are constantly looking outside for solutions or reasons for the various challenges we face, and yet most of them emerge from the six inches between our ears. The way our brain develops as we grow up creates unavoidable limitations, which in turn create so much of the dysfunction that is common in family business. The way the human brain develops, not lack of business acumen, is the reason why family business so often falls prey to the curse – rags to riches and back again in three generations.

'Let me explain …

'Human beings are driven by the biological imperative – our drive to survive. The definition of the biological imperative is the "need of living organisms to perpetuate their existence". It includes the following hierarchy of logical imperatives for a living organism: survival, territorialism, competition, reproduction, quality of life–seeking and group forming.[4] Interestingly, when diagnosing the challenges in family business, the issues ultimately fall under one of these subconscious and hardwired drivers.

'We are intrinsically wired to find and consume food, defend territory, congregate in groups, find a partner and produce children. We are not naturally wired to do just about anything else – including business.

'Although human beings today inhabit a world that bears almost no resemblance to the one inhabited by our Stone Age ancestors, we are still navigating this new world with the ingrained mentality and instinctive drives Stone Age hunter-gatherers possessed. For example, finding food used to be a daily problem fraught with all manner of potentially lethal dangers, from toxic berries to sabre-toothed tigers. Today we go to the supermarket, or order online and someone will deliver food to our door. And yet, in the intervening 200,000 years or so, we've had marginal, if any, biological or neurological upgrades. Hence Professor Nicholson's statement, "You can take the person out of the Stone Age, but you can't take the Stone Age out of the person."[5]

'This is the core of any problem – including the ones you are facing now in your business.'

John asked, 'Are you trying to tell us that the problems we need your help with are not really business problems at all, they are people problems or human problems?'

'Yes – that's exactly what I'm saying,' said the advisor. 'Clearly there are business issues you need to address, but until you address the human stuff, nothing will change. Remember I told you that we are not "born ready", and the process to ready occurs through something called conditioning?'

John and Ayesha nodded their heads (looking somewhat sceptical!).

'Okay ... what is "not ready" is our brain. When a human baby is born their brain is around 350 cc in size. Any larger and you jeopardise survival of the species. But, to be considered "ready", a human being needs a much bigger brain than the one they are born with so growth after birth becomes paramount. The typical human brain will therefore grow another 1,000 cc at least. In terms of mass, most of that additional growth will occur before the age of four or five years old.[6] In terms of capability, the growth and development will occur over a couple of decades. In fact, the human brain isn't fully "ready" until we reach our early to mid-20s.'

'Really – that late?' exclaimed John.

'Yes – it's crazy, right!' said the advisor. 'We think we are adults at 18 years old and legally we are, but the neocortex, which plays such a crucial role in high-order brain function, isn't even finished until *after* we leave university or several years into our first job! This includes sensory perception, conscious thought, reasoning, problem solving, decision making, understanding and using language, learning, memory and emotional regulation.'

Standing up, the advisor retrieved a diagram that he passed to John and Ayesha. The advisor continued, 'From an evolutionary perspective, our brain consists of three areas – the reptilian brain, the midbrain (also known as the mammalian brain or limbic system) and the neocortex ... '

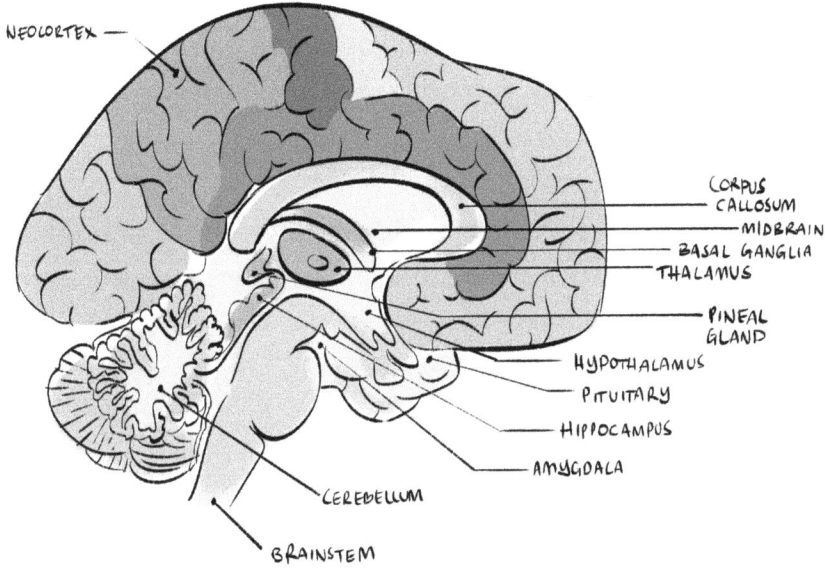

'The purpose of conditioning is to learn quickly, and part of that learning is to assess incoming signals, determine whether those signals pose a threat and classify that information for later use. This process is facilitated by the amygdala – the body's emotional early warning system. And while the neocortex is far from ready at birth, the amygdala is fully functional at birth. The amygdala *is* born ready. It's alerting us to danger before the part of the brain we use to recognise ourselves is even active!

'From an evolutionary psychology perspective, this associative learning model is referred to as *classification before calculus*.[7] In an effort to make sense of changing and uncertain events and circumstances, the human brain classifies all experiences instantaneously so that in the future it doesn't have to calculate whether the information is important or not – that's why they become thinking shortcuts. Because of the sheer volume of information in our modern environment, this skill has become extremely well-honed, and we have developed prodigious capabilities for sorting, classifying and deleting information.

'This ability to classify everything in a nanosecond has always been central to our survival as a species – whether to eat the red berries or the blue ones, and who in the tribe to align with. Instantaneous assessment of people still occurs today as we make immediate judgements about everyone we meet.

'And this ability to classify without thinking is the biological basis of the default settings we create. Essentially, these are predetermined conclusions that are formed and stored from past thoughts and experiences. They free us from having to consciously process most of the data we receive in the present.

'In theory, this is an amazing superpower of human evolution. In practice, however, it's a recipe for disaster. We think we are making decisions based on logic and reason when the truth is, we are simply reacting to long-forgotten events or situations that were sufficiently challenging that they created a default setting to help us avoid the same or a similar event in the future.

'There are two types of conditioning,' added the advisor, 'single trial and multiple trial. As the name suggests, single-trial conditioning occurs because of a single exposure to a stimulus. The most obvious example is when a child burns her fingers on a stove.

'Do either of you remember a situation with one of your children where they burnt their finger when they were small?' asked the advisor.

'Yes, I do,' replied Ayesha, 'I remember being in the kitchen with Nathan. I can't remember what I was doing, but I turned my back for two seconds and Nathan was up on his tiptoes next to the frying pan. By the time I turned back, he had burnt his finger, and I was yelling at him to get away from the stove.'

'Okay, what happened in that moment was single-trial conditioning. The physical pain and corresponding emotional pain of being yelled at was enough to burn that learning into Nathan's brain.'

Noting that Ayesha looked sad, the advisor added, 'Don't feel bad – this means he didn't have to repeat the event and therefore re-experience the pain, ensuring his safety and survival into the future. Science has proven a correlation between the number of "markers" that occur in an event or situation and the creation of learning. The more markers – such as fear, pain or environmental or situational data points – that are involved, the greater the fusion of neural patterns and the faster the learning.[8]

'Essentially, in that learning moment at the stove, Nathan's brain scanned the environment and collected all the information that set the moment apart, recorded it and classified it. Nathan probably doesn't even remember this incident and he certainly wasn't aware of what his brain was doing, but it logged everything from what you were wearing when you shouted at him, to what was on the radio in the background, to what he was wearing, to the temperature in the room, to who else was present, to any smells and sounds that could be identified. What his brain was doing was cataloguing the event to map its characteristics and parameters, so it could alert him to danger should a cluster of those same or similar parameters appear again in a future situation. Remember, "what fires together wires together" – so these disparate characteristics of the episode are forever connected or wired together, thus ensuring ongoing safety, survival and pain avoidance.

'The second type of conditioning is multiple-trial conditioning. It is often less dramatic or memorable, but its impact is every bit as powerful. Again, as the name would suggest, it relates to things learned through repetition. Essentially, when we are told something enough times, or we experience something enough times, whether our frontal lobe believes it or not, it has a formative impact on us.

'Like every family, you all have plenty of default settings created through multiple-trial conditioning to contend with – it's inevitable. For example, Christopher has probably received the message from you John that he's a bit "soft".'

'I've never said anything like that,' said John defensively.

'Sounds like you don't need to,' added Ayesha. 'Nathan has certainly picked up that nothing is ever quite right for "St Christopher",' as she made air quotes.

'You have to remember this is not conscious,' reminded the advisor. 'We talked about it earlier, but Priya's consistent messaging was that she wasn't quite as good as the boys. She played sport so she could get closer to you, John, but your own conditioning meant you never saw past her gender. The list will go on and on.

'And while these stereotypes translate into playful or even loving monikers in the family, when that family is in business together, they can be incredibly unhelpful. They are essentially default settings created by multiple-trial conditioning, where family members are markers of the default. And, of course, those family members are the same people everyone is now trying to run a business with! Every family member takes on a role in that family: the joker, the black sheep, the difficult one, the aggressive one. For family members who are not in business together, these defaults become the fodder for the clinical psychologist they may visit later in life. Or they are the reason Christmas is so fraught with old spats re-energised over prosecco and tiramisu. But when these defaults are "trapped" inside a shared business, it's like putting them in a kiln – they become baked in!

'Imagine a business meeting with various key players attending. You are chairing the meeting, John, and Christopher, Nathan and Priya are involved. Christopher is making an important point and Nathan says, "Okay, St Christopher, no need to get your knickers in a knot." How does that change the meeting? How does Christopher feel? Is that likely to get the best thinking out of the group? Would Nathan say that to an unrelated colleague? He might, but I'm guessing he'd never dream of directing such a statement towards an *employee* – and yet he feels totally comfortable directing it towards his *brother*. Is Christopher going to bring his A-game or is he going to simmer with resentment? He may look like the 35-year-old that entered the meeting half an hour earlier, but physiologically, emotionally and intellectually he's not.

'He's been emotionally transported back to the countless fights he had as a young child: fighting with his younger but physically bigger brother in their shared bedroom; fights that would involve Nathan criticising Christopher's creativity and basically bullying his older brother. Nathan's "funny" comment about the knickers triggers a default setting that has been running since they were children and neither of them even realises it.

'The overriding emotion he feels may be rage, but his response to this rage is withdrawal. While everyone at the table is laughing at Nathan's comment, Christopher has shut down. If you were in the meeting too, Ayesha, you would notice that Christopher scowls at his brother, sits down and doesn't speak again. He can no longer think straight. His physiology is on high alert, and he's probably experiencing a surge of the stress hormone – cortisol. It doesn't matter if he tries to tell himself that Nathan is being his usual painful self; the threat signal has already been actioned by the amygdala, which shuts down access to the neocortex and readies the body for fight, flight or freeze. His withdrawal is his biological freeze response based on years of similar situations since he was a kid.

'If Christopher's conditioning had been different and he and his brother were closer or had a more balanced relationship he would have laughed, too, then dismissed Nathan's comment and carried on with his presentation – but that didn't happen because of the emotion stirred up by the amygdala to "help Christopher survive".

'How we feel at any given moment will have a large impact on how we perceive what is happening around us. What we perceive as reality is subjective. It is an emotion-fuelled interpretation, as evidenced by Christopher in the meeting.

'Just think about this for a moment. It certainly helps to explain why we witness so many sparks in the workplace – angry meetings, tantrums in the boardroom, sulking after performance reviews or storming out of meetings. In many very real ways, emotion is what makes us human, and yet it is often expected that as soon as we enter the workplace, we somehow turn this human characteristic off. We don't.

We *can't*. And that is true regardless of gender. Emotion comes with us wherever we go, and as a result, it influences our perception of events and can seriously interfere with our thinking.

'This is challenging enough in normal everyday life,' said the advisor, 'but attempt to run a successful family business within that context and these human characteristics can derail things remarkably quickly – as evidenced by the frequency that rags to riches and back again occurs in just three generations. A huge number of our conditioned responses and default settings are created before we are six years old. As a result, almost all of them involve our parents and siblings, who become markers that, along with the presence of other markers received via our five senses, trigger a response in later life. As a result, our amygdala is sounding the alarm on an almost daily basis in a family business because we are working with the guy who stuck a pencil in our ear when we were three years old! This doesn't happen anywhere near as often in non-family business settings because family is not involved. Of course, everyone has default settings, it's just they are not as frequently triggered because one of the markers, a family member, is not in the working environment.

'As we grow up, we grow into a role or stereotype based on myriad factors and influences. It doesn't matter how old we are: as soon as the family is together again, each parent and child will take on their role – forever pigeonholed as "the baby" or "St Christopher" or "aggressive". That's hard enough in a family setting; it can be infuriating, condescending and humiliating in a family business setting.

'Often these conditioned responses hijack our best thinking, making business success even more unlikely. Let's look at the potential outcome of Nathan's finger-burning incident, for example. Say Nathan manages to secure a meeting with a prospect, but it can only happen on Sunday. Nathan agrees and they arrange to meet in a local café. Nathan decides to have the meeting and then go to the gym, so he grabs a blue fleece top, as it's a cold day. The prospect arrives wearing jeans and a red t-shirt, and they order coffee and sit down. The radio in the café is playing in the background, and the DJ is inviting listeners to "guess the year" of the song; then "I don't like Mondays" starts playing. For some reason, Nathan feels off. He was really excited about this meeting, but now he's filled with foreboding that he can't explain. He presses on and makes his pitch, but he doesn't seem to be getting through to the prospect. Nathan's brain goes into overdrive: "What was I thinking? I should have dressed smarter than this – I look like an amateur." Nathan rationalises the outcome and assumes the meeting didn't go well because he wasn't prepared and, with hindsight, he was dressed inappropriately – but actually, it didn't go well because several of the markers that wired together when he was four years old and burnt his finger were activated in the café and that default setting put him on edge and made him feel the way he did when his mother shouted at him for getting too close to the stove! His amygdala sounded the alarm, which simultaneously shut down access to his frontal lobe and readied him for a survival response. A tad over the top considering he was having a chat with a possible client in a café! Without access to the thinking part of the brain, the presentation was awkward – Nathan effectively froze, and later blamed the aberration on the fact that he was dressed too casually.'

'But that's ridiculous!' said John and Ayesha together.

'Yes, it is – but it's also scientific fact. You must remember that the subconscious mind is vastly more powerful than the conscious mind. All these learnings happened before we had the brain capability and horsepower to determine if something that was wired together and fired together should be connected or whether it was accurate or helpful.

'Human beings mistake the work of the midbrain as being "I", when it is in fact "I robot" or perhaps more accurately, "AI robot". One of the most extraordinary characteristics of artificial intelligence (AI) is its speed at data assessment and the application of algorithms. And yet our amygdala is almost as fast and equally capable of instantly matching the vast repository of internal nonsense we accumulate during the conditioning process to any manner of external nonsense, arriving at a conclusion before the thinking brain is even in gear.

'The faulty explanations we then use to explain that nonsense is an example of something called "ethnomethodology" – the study of the methods we use to understand life and make sense of our experiences. Developed by sociologist Harold Garfinkel, ethnomethodology upends the idea that "everything happens for a reason" and states instead that stuff happens and then we rationalise it and explain it to ourselves so that it makes sense.[9]

'This is what we are up against! Of course, having a business that includes family members can make the business more personal, inspiring and meaningful. It can also make it more fun. But if we don't first appreciate the human dynamics at play, trouble is inevitable. The mere presence of a family member can trigger all sorts of long-forgotten memories, feelings, reactions and default settings, polluting our ability to access our best thinking and smartest decisions. This can and does result in arguments, resentments or the emergence of familiar behaviour patterns and family stereotypes that are counterproductive to business success and personal happiness.

'I also need to explain some misconceptions about happiness, but maybe this is a good time to break for the day and regroup tomorrow. It's been a lot to take in,' said the advisor.

'It certainly has,' said Ayesha. 'It makes sense, but I'm just really shocked that so many of the issues we are facing are human issues and not business or even family issues.'

'Yes,' replied the advisor. 'But the good news is that once you understand these human issues, the business issues become much easier to solve.'

'Before you go, let's just recap so you can discuss and consider these things over dinner. What is happening in your business right now is not really a business issue. It's a homo sapiens issue. The way our brain develops from "not ready" at birth to "ready" is through a learning process called conditioning. And although it is a human superpower, it is blunt, wildly inaccurate and all the learning is done before we have the brain capability to determine whether it is accurate or helpful, which isn't great! The result is a bunch of default settings or automatic responses, biases and prejudices that we believe as "fact" which may not be. And because most of that learning happened when we were very young, one of the markers for the defaults being triggered is family members, which can be especially challenging in a family business. But it is all manageable when we understand these limitations and implement a process that nullifies their negative impacts.

'So go and get some rest and I'll see you back here bright-eyed and bushy-tailed tomorrow, when we can unpack some of the misconceptions around happiness.'

Third Meeting: Understanding Happiness

'I hope you had a chance to relax a little last night,' enquired the advisor.

'It was good, thanks, and nice to have some time to consider what you have told us,' said John. 'It makes so much sense, and we could both remember examples when one of our kids seemed to overreact to something. Now we know why! It also makes me wonder if I haven't been a little quick to judgement, and maybe it's been my default setting steering the bus rather than me!'

'Almost certainly,' said the advisor, 'but don't worry too much about it – none of us can escape this, we just have to understand it better and plot a path through.

'From the sounds of things, part of the reason you both feel stuck is that when you started the business, the plan was to create something that provided for your family, and you had the opportunity to do something that made you happy. It sounds like you really love construction – would that be fair to say?'

Both John and Ayesha nodded their agreement.

'I never really thought how our lives might change if the business became successful. Even if it crossed my mind, I just assumed it would be a great problem to have,' John added sadly.

'We thought life would become more certain and simpler as the wealth grew,' added Ayesha, 'but it seems we were wrong about that too. Although we don't really understand why.'

Again, the advisor took a seat beside the couple. 'If it makes you feel any better – you are not alone. By the time I meet the individual members of a family business, issues will already have started to arise, or there will be a recognition that problems are imminent. Often these family businesses are extremely successful and have generated significant wealth. When I listen to these families, they are always wrestling with the juxtaposition of two distinct things – the *family* and the *business* – and how to make each work without damaging the other. This is *not easy*. Often, they are seeking to measure, monitor or better understand the impact the business and its resulting wealth is having on the family and its ongoing connectedness. In other words, the founder is increasingly aware that the business, together with the resulting wealth, is causing uncertainty and complexity issues or will cause issues that they did not anticipate when they started the business. And those issues are impacting individual and collective happiness.'

Standing again to return to the whiteboard, the advisor explained, 'Study after study has repeatedly demonstrated that quality of life and happiness depend on two factors: how we experience work, and our relationships with others (our connectedness).[10]

'Of course, how a G2 experiences work in a family business is often challenging. Too often they are not taken seriously by G1 or by other senior non-family members of the team; or they are never quite sure of their place – whether they should be there or deserve to be there. I'm not saying that is the case with you, but if it is – it's remarkably common.'

'No, I can see those issues in our situation. I can see the confusion between Christopher, Nathan and Priya, but it's also starting to affect key members of staff who seem to want to know what I plan to do too, and I know for a fact that a few people think Nathan is a loose cannon,' explained John.

'As I said, it's inevitable,' reassured the advisor. 'Let me explain ... Psychologists Richard Ryan and Edward Deci proposed self-determination theory (SDT), which outlines what we need to feel motivated and happy: competence, autonomy and relatedness.[11] According to Ryan and Deci, we need to be able to demonstrate competence in our daily activities; we need to have some level of control and autonomy over our work and lives; and we need to feel connected to others we care about. Again, we can see the potential problems that arise in the peculiar hothouse of family business. The confusion family members often feel about why they are in the business eats away at their perceived levels of competence. Are they there because they are good at their role, or are they there because of their surname? This competence issue is also almost always questioned by non-family employees. Autonomy is also missing or at least intermittent, as the founder holds on to control. Often, G1 will not think G2 are ready or capable enough and will deliberately limit their autonomy because of it. And relatedness is complicated because connectedness is often with other family members that may not get on very well, such as Nathan and Christopher. In many ways, family business creates an environment that makes competence, autonomy and relatedness very hard to achieve. Which obviously has a knock-on effect on motivation and happiness.'

'That makes so much sense!' exclaimed Ayesha. 'And I can see this play out for all our children in different ways. It feels like Priya and Christopher have almost given up and that they are already pulling away. None of them seems happy right now! Please tell me there is a solution.'

'Relax, there is absolutely a solution,' said the advisor. 'But before we get to it, the situation also gets a lot more complex because of money. Far from being a balm to the issues of motivation and happiness, money becomes an accelerant to escalating conflict and potential hostility.'

'No shit!' said John. 'We have recognised that ourselves but again we just don't understand why.'

'Okay, let me explain ... If unmanaged or taken for granted, money can work against motivation and happiness. Having money doesn't always help people develop competence, because those with money are not forced to forge their own path and earn a living the way those from non-wealthy families are. You said yourself that Nathan and Anika's experience in the family was different to that of Christopher and Priya because of the changing economic reality of the business. This is normal, but it can have unexpected consequences. In many cases, people from wealthy families never really achieve autonomy because they always have the financial safety net of the family wealth, and may even be paid an allowance well into later life.'

'Have you ever watched the TV show *Succession*?' asked the advisor.

John and Ayesha said they have and the advisor went on, 'One of my favourite scenes is when the oldest son, Connor Roy, who has managed to blow through millions on various fancies such as funding a play for his girlfriend and running for President of the United States, pulls Logan aside in the final episode of the second series. They are on the family yacht, and he asks for a small injection of $100 million. It's a TV show, but this is not fiction for many mega-wealthy families. Also, children of wealthy families often suffer from a lack of relatedness because they are never really sure if others are interested in *them*, or in gaining access to their parents or their share of the family wealth.'

'Yeah, but we are not in that league,' argued Ayesha.

'I appreciate that, but it doesn't matter,' said the advisor. 'You have created significant wealth, and while your children may never ask for a small injection of $100 million, there are unspoken, undiscussed concerns and questions about that wealth that are impacting their happiness. Not to mention the guilt they feel at thinking about it in the first place!

'The most compelling reason happiness remains so elusive is we don't appreciate the two enemies of happiness that impact us all, regardless of our economic situation, how we experience work or even our connectedness: uncertainty and complexity.

'Like the impact of the way we grow up and brain development, what is not understood or even really considered is that uncertainty and complexity are especially challenging at either extreme of the wealth continuum.'

'What do you mean?' asked John.

'John, come up to the whiteboard for a moment. If I draw a graph with uncertainty on one axis and wealth on the other, what do you think the relationship is? In other words, when there is no money where is the uncertainty, and how does that relationship change when there is more money?'

John approached the whiteboard and after a moment or two drew the following graph …

A SUCCESSION BLUEPRINT

'Okay great work,' said the advisor. 'This assumption is logical – uncertainty is bound to be greatest when someone has no money – but it is another example of Mencken's assertion that for every complex problem there is an answer that is clear, simple and wrong.

'This is the real relationship between money and uncertainty … ' and the advisor proceeded to create a new graph on the whiteboard.

'It is true that there is a huge amount of uncertainty when someone has no money. The worry is around where it is coming from, whether there is enough, and what will happen if there is a price rise or an unexpected bill. This is not fun. That uncertainty decreases with wealth to a point of "having enough" to meet all their needs and a little extra for any possible surprises. That is the point of low uncertainty. Life is manageable. Beyond that, however, uncertainty increases again as wealth increases. Now the uncertainty is around what to do with it, how to use it wisely, and how to look after it. It's an uncertainty minefield! The key point to remember here is that for your children, it's the "not knowing" what their relationship with the wealth is, or whether there is a relationship that drives the uncertainty,' added the advisor.

'What would happen,' asked the advisor, 'if you as a family always followed three rules:

1. You collectively engage in a rational assessment of what "enough" means (revisited every 10 years).
2. Each generation is always entitled to have "enough" as defined by 1.
3. Each generation must ensure that the next generation also has "enough".

'Do you think that would reduce the uncertainty?' asked the advisor.

'Absolutely,' said John and Ayesha in unison.

'Okay great. Now it's your turn, Ayesha,' said the advisor. 'Can you come up to the whiteboard and have a stab at the relationship between wealth and complexity? If I draw a graph where one axis is complexity and the other is wealth, what do you think the relationship is? In other words, when there is no money, what is the complexity like, and when there is more money, what does that do to complexity?'

Ayesha slowly got up and approached the whiteboard, and drew the following graph ...

'There is very little to no complexity when someone has no money,' explained Ayesha. 'Those who are struggling to survive are just struggling to survive. That is their sole focus. But once wealth grows, so does complexity. What do we do with it? How should it be invested? Where do we save it? Who has access to it? But I'm assuming that past a certain point, complexity tails off again. Because serious wealth makes life so much easier – right?'

'But does it?' asked the advisor. 'Has that been true for you?'

'Well ... no,' acknowledged Ayesha, 'but I thought you meant the sort of wealth that billionaires have.'

The advisor replied, 'Whatever way you want to look at this, my understanding is that you have created significant wealth, well into the millions. Whether you are billionaires is irrelevant. Has the money made your life more or less complex?'

'More complex, especially lately!' said John.

'Of course it has, because now there are so many unanswered questions. The real relationship between complexity and wealth is ... '

Having drawn the new graph on the whiteboard, the advisor said, 'The truth is that uncertainty and complexity make happiness as elusive for the very poor as for the very rich. Uncertainty and complexity can also play havoc with how we experience work (autonomy and competence) *and* our connectedness, which is the real source of happiness and family longevity.

'Happiness, certainly in a family business context, often comes down to the ability of the family to stay connected as well as feeling individually and collectively supported, whether inside or outside the business. The irony is that, contrary to popular belief, wealth can make happiness less likely in this scenario. When faced with this uncomfortable reality, founders find it surprising and alarming. That isn't how it's supposed to be!'

'We can already see this happening. This is why we are so desperate for a solution,' said John. 'Everyone in the business is experiencing a huge amount of uncertainty. I know I have to make some decisions, but as far as I'm concerned, there is no heir apparent. And I don't want to cause a rift in the family, which seems unavoidable right now. I'm also reluctant to step back because I'm uncertain about whether any of my kids have the ability to ensure the business continues to be a success, never mind take it to the next level.'

'I'm also uncertain about whether I will ever get John to step back so we can enjoy the wealth we have created together and pass the mantle on to our children,' lamented Ayesha. 'What's the point in creating wealth if everyone is too strung out to enjoy any of it? The children are, of course, no longer children. All in their late 20s and 30s, they are as uncertain now about what their dad plans to do with the business as they ever were.'

'And remember, we all default to the worst outcome,' added the advisor. 'I promise you this uncertainty and corresponding lack of information is also activating their innate pessimism and they all, to one extent or another, are imagining the worst probable outcome.

'They have all grown up inside the bubble of the business and benefited from the wealth that business has created, but the uncertainty around whether they should be, could be or want to be in the business has robbed them of genuine autonomy and consequently direction, drive and happiness. They are uncertain, and the options are complex. They are confused about the wealth, which further amplifies the pessimism. They know there is money, but do they have access to it? Are they entitled to it? What are the rules? What are the expectations? For the most part, they have no idea. And that uncertainty in the G2s is almost certainly creating tension in their own families. Is it causing arguments with their own partners and their siblings, which further strains the connectedness and diminishes happiness?

'You both look very despondent, so before I explain the twin enemies of happiness, be assured there is a solution and we will get to it next,' added the advisor.

'Right now, you just have to understand that it's very hard to be happy if there are important things in or around our lives that are shrouded in mystery, about which we feel uncertain. It may appear counterintuitive, especially to those without wealth, but appreciating the role of uncertainty can help us understand why wealth *can* and often *does* create unhappiness.

'Wealth brings with it a whole new level of uncertainty,' added the advisor, 'about whether it will be looked after, who will get it, when everyone will get it, how much will they get, whether that is considered "fair" whatever the hell that means, what the responsibilities and obligations to the wealth are – the uncertainty is endless. And, of course, this uncertainty is fertiliser for the default settings we discussed earlier.

'The minute a family accumulates significant wealth, such as you have, a new level of uncertainty is created. I've worked with a number of G2s who are unable to commit to a career path or develop the autonomy and competence so essential for happiness because of that uncertainty. They believe that sooner or later, whatever path they choose will be disrupted or compromised by the need to manage wealth or the expectation that they manage wealth. In other words, they may want to work outside the family business and become a lawyer but they know that even if they invest their time in that pursuit and are "allowed" to become a lawyer there will come a time where they will be tapped on the shoulder and expected to return to the family business in whatever way necessary. This wouldn't be so destructive if they were able to be a lawyer in the business, but this is not always the case. You probably recognise this scenario with Christopher. He chose architecture to win favour with you, John, and has his own business, but he feels that at some point you are going to pull him back into the business full time, and his aspirations will be pushed aside. Is that possible?'

'Well, yes, but it wouldn't be like that,' defended John.

'You might not want it to be like that,' added Ayesha. 'But I promise you, that is exactly what it's going to feel like for Christopher.'

'This is not about looking for blame or anything like that. It's just about being realistic about expectations and understanding the complexity of the situation, so don't beat yourselves up about any of this. Besides, it's not always the G1s that are creating the problems.

'I have also met a lot of G2s who are not prepared to commit to a career path because their true desire is to be responsible for managing the wealth, but there is no clear pathway to that outcome or certainty that a role even exists for them. Or the G2s simply believe the family business is the easy option – but it rarely is! Whatever the reason, G2s are often stuck in limbo – they know there are some expectations and obligations on them but are not clear about what those expectations and obligations are, or whether they even want them.

'It's also interesting to note,' added the advisor, 'that other words for certainty in family include *discipline* and *rules* (governance). There is a clear correlation between a happy kid and a kid who must abide by certain rules and who is certain of their limitations. Ironically, less well-off families tend to be better at tough love than their wealthier counterparts. They must be: the children must pull their weight in the home for it to function. You already said this was your own experience before the business started to do well. When you were not as wealthy, your children learned the meaning of the word "no" because money constraints demanded it. To their detriment, wealthy families don't have the same constraints and consequently have fewer rules, which, in turn, amplifies the uncertainty and helps to breed entitlement and unhappiness. When a child grows up getting everything they want without responsibility or accountability, they can find it very hard to know where their natural abilities lie and therefore what could or might make them genuinely happy. That doesn't appear to have happened with you, but it is very common.'

'I'm not so sure it hasn't happened to us,' said John. 'Certainly there is a feeling among the children that we treated them differently.'

THIRD MEETING: UNDERSTANDING HAPPINESS

'None of this is easy,' added the advisor. 'Don't beat yourselves up about it. What matters is that unless you take constructive and conscious action to wrestle that complexity into some agreed rules and order, the outcome is assured: rags to riches and back again in three generations.

'When it comes to family business, there are three domains or circles.'

'Each of the three circles represents one of the dynamics in a family business that needs to be considered because it adds a new layer of uncertainty and complexity to the mix.

'First there's the family circle,' the advisor explained. 'Family, to borrow Kurt Vonnegut's reference to history, presents us with "nothing more than a list of surprises [and] prepares [us] for nothing more than to be surprised yet again."[12] I would go further and say that family relationships are the only relationships we have that can withstand these surprises without eventually breaking down. Although I have seen that breakdown enough to know it does and can happen.'

'I suppose,' added Ayesha, 'family is the constant audience in front of which we experience the ups and downs of our lives.'

'Exactly,' said the advisor. 'Those experiences often complicate our family relationships. If we are lucky, family is also one of the most rewarding parts of life, offering us lifelong connectedness to people we care about. Our family circle represents our first "tribe": our place of comfort and safety against the outside world. It is the place where we are loved no matter what – at least that's the theory. Our family members often know us better than we know ourselves, but there is a downside to that familiarity that can be infuriating.

'The familiarity we feel towards each other as family members means we say things to each other and react emotionally to each other in ways that we would never dream of in a different setting. Again, this adds to the complexity of these relationships. Many families have their own language too, which can confuse things yet further. Because we are family, we assume that other members of the family will be mind-readers, so we often engage in less communication, not more. This is a mistake.'

'Yeah, we learned that the hard way with Anika's restaurant,' said John. 'I just assumed that everyone would realise that it was a loan. But I should have made that much clearer from the outset.'

'It's a common problem,' added the advisor. 'We think that being family makes everything easier and in some ways it does, but it also makes it much harder and in need of more detailed communication, not less. And because you are family and all grew up inside that bubble, you are certainly not able to be subjective and objective at the same time. In fact, everyone in the business, including family members, will seek to find data or information that supports their pre-existing default settings and seek to present that to the rest of the group as objective fact. It's not. It's cherry-picking data so they can present their entirely subjective opinion as objective fact.'

'Nathan did that recently,' said John. 'He had done some research on how much architects cost per hour and what the industry benchmark was, and tried to get me to agree that Christopher was therefore being overpaid. But he had got the benchmark rate for the Northern Territory and not New South Wales, and he was not accounting for the fact that Christopher was also bringing interior design input to the build. It was nonsense and yet he presented it as "objective fact".'

'That's a great example of what I'm talking about here,' said the advisor.

'Every family will have factions and cliques. Some siblings will like each other more than others, as evidenced by Nathan and Christopher. Just because a group of people is a family doesn't mean that everyone will like everyone else to the same degree. They may all love each other, but chances are there will be alliances and friendships within the family group. That's just the nature of family.

'The dynamics, however, also generate additional complexity. Things like the age gap between the children, gender difference, birth order, cultural differences in the parents, number of children, the presence of twins, second families and blended families all play a role.[13] And you are certainly wrestling with some of these complexities,' said the advisor.

'In his book *Stewardship in Your Family Enterprise*, author Dennis Jaffe shared the universal family dramas.[14] This includes the common conflict between the founder and their children. This is true regardless of founder gender. The founder may say they want succession and may encourage their children's involvement in the business but the route towards that outcome is rarely smooth. As the founder gets older and the children become more confident in their own abilities and opinions, conflict is almost inevitable. I'm not saying this is relevant to you John,' added the advisor, 'but often vanity and ego mean the founder becomes reluctant to step aside.'

'I see you smirking, Ayesha,' said John. 'But to be fair, there is some truth in what you are saying. And I can certainly feel the conflict escalating within the kids and between them and me for different reasons.'

'My point here is not to insinuate this is your fault, John,' added the advisor, 'it's to make you aware that it's just the normal course of family business – unless you step in and change course. Often, founders end up undermining their children and plotting against them to hold on to power. They are often not even conscious of doing it. Conversely, the children might start plotting against the founder. This is especially common between sons and fathers, and you have indicated this is already happening to some extent.'

'Yes, although there is no way Christopher and Nathan would plot together on anything!' said John.

'By the sounds of things, that seems unlikely, but there is still complexity in the situation. The children may know that they will inherit at some point, but they already feel that they are being forced to wait in the wings, promised various enticements to keep them "in play". However, if you are like most founders, these enticements rarely materialise, which in turn fosters even greater resentment and negatively impacts connectedness and relatedness. The children stay, but don't have any real power or authority, and they know it. This means they often feel as though they have zero autonomy or ways of demonstrating competence – both essential for happiness. Plenty is talked about in terms of succession, but it never happens. Instead, the founder drags their heels until the day they drop dead and all hell breaks loose.'

John and Ayesha look at each other – it's clear this has hit a nerve.

'Sorry,' said the advisor, 'that might sound a bit harsh, but it's a fact.

'If we look for a moment at your construction business … the business itself would be challenging enough because of all the things that need to be considered and actioned. All the supplier relationships, and the relationship with the bank, can and do change with the prevailing economic conditions. Property ownership is also something that politics gets involved with; policy affects who can buy and invest in property in Australia. This can and does change depending on which political party is in power. This changes the demand in the market, which can diminish profitability and alter the viability of development projects. The pipeline needs to be managed very closely to ensure that enough money is being made by the business, the projects are progressing on time and on budget, and the people employed by the business are doing their jobs to the highest standard. If something falls through the cracks, additional pressure comes to bear. Deadlines and supplier issues can cause delays and budget blowouts. Lawyers get involved – complexity on steroids all by itself.

'Now throw family into the mix and the scope for complexity increases a hundredfold. Long-serving, loyal employees who have helped to build the business can very easily get their noses out of joint if one of the children is introduced as your 2IC. It does not matter that Christopher and Priya studied relevant degrees at university or that Nathan worked his way up in the business. There will always be people who say they are only there because of their surname. Even if they do a great job, they will always be resented by some. G2s can rarely win in business. They are either unprepared, so employees resent it, or they are forced into the job, so they resent it. Even if they are prepared, want the job and do it brilliantly, some employees will *still* resent them.'

'You've already noticed that, haven't you, John – a few long-term employees making the odd comment,' added Ayesha.

As John nodded in agreement, the advisor continued, 'As for your kids, they are still as confused as ever by the family and business complexity. They are not sure what is expected of them. They don't know who you really favour to take over, and even if there was a role for them, they are now unsure if they want it. Often, these types of crucial discussions just don't happen. They will be ignored until something happens to you. Plus, without you at the helm to steady the succession ship, it can be devastating to the business and the family. The good news for you is you are seeking a solution now!

'Remember,' said the advisor, 'business is not the open plains of the savannah. It holds its own dangers, but for the most part we can get through each day without facing mortal danger. As a result, our amygdala is almost certainly overreacting in this environment and alerting us to dangers that simply do not exist, which ironically leaves us even more exposed to the dangers that do exist! What we need is a way to get the neocortex into the conversation and keep it switched on. Of course, the presence of family members in that discussion means defaults are often running wild so the thinking part of the brain is AWOL.

'Don't get me wrong,' added the advisor. 'Families can be wonderful and make events, occasions and normal everyday life so much better, but put them inside a commercial enterprise and they can cause havoc.

'And as you have created a significant measure of success, you now also have to contend with the complexity created by wealth,' explained the advisor. 'Groucho Marx once said, "While money can't buy happiness, it certainly lets you choose your own form of misery." Wealth may be the universal yardstick of success, it may be what we go into business to create, but once the business starts to generate significant wealth, that wealth invites additional complexity. It may solve some problems, but it also creates even more new ones, many of which are anything but easy.

'When the wealth is generated inside a family business, the complexity goes through the roof because of a whole new set of issues. What are the rules for distribution? Is there a G2 who is best placed to manage the money? Does that person have the necessary qualifications and experience? How comfortable do the other members of the family feel about that? What is that person's risk profile in relation to the risk profile of the other members of the family whose wealth that person is managing? Each person has a natural disposition towards risk that can radically alter their opinion – not only within the business and its focus, but also in terms of wealth management. In a wealthy family business, there are often pools of money being governed and yet even something as simple as a risk profile creates an infinite number of possible portfolio allocation strategies. I have met many families where the root cause of many of their internal business and family issues was a difference in risk profile between the family members in the business. Unless recognised and addressed, this difference can be extremely destructive.

'In family wealth, the usual stereotypes and default settings also come into play. How would Christopher, Priya and Nathan feel if you decided to involve Anika more in the business and assigned her the role of managing the family wealth? It's not her passion, and a qualification from a French culinary school isn't going to cut it, regardless of her surname. Each generation will also almost certainly feel differently about the various types of investments.

'Money can do very strange things to people, largely because it triggers the survival response, and people can become selfish, scared or demanding. People with significant generational wealth can very easily lose their sense of reality. There are now whole industries dedicated to helping the wealthy part with their cash via outrageous gifts and experiences – everything from gold cars to famous footballers showing up for a kid's birthday party. So wealth is also very complex.

'But, put that wealth in a family and the complexity ratchets up significantly,' added the advisor. 'How much is there? Will I receive any? If so, how much? What will I need to do to be entitled to that? Does my surname entitle me to some of it without effort or involvement in the business? Should the distribution be the same for those involved in the business and those not? Who decides? Money creates tensions and causes arguments. And of course, it's considered impolite in most societies to talk about money, so the conversations that are so needed about wealth either never happen or happen too late. This lack of knowledge triggers the greatest default of all, being that everyone jumps to the worst probable conclusion. Emotion enters the picture as everyone wants to know but is scared to ask. Worries emerge about whether distribution is fair or equitable. If one sibling gets something, do all the siblings get the same?

'When you put all this together,' continued the advisor, 'and someone makes the observation, "Wow, that family really screwed things up!" no one should be surprised. The only correct response to such an observation is "Of course they did – they were human beings trying to build a skyscraper without scaffolding. It's amazing more people were not hurt!"

'Whether you realise it or not, John, until now you have been that scaffolding, and what you've created is impressive – make no mistake. But,' warned the advisor, 'as soon as something happens to you, that scaffolding will come crashing down. And if the business is halfway through building level 15, the whole thing will collapse. Never mind having to deal with the grief of that loss, but it's also likely that the strategy for the business would be lost too.

'This constantly escalating pressure of complexity should lead us to the conclusion that we ought not to be surprised when success and wealth become the undoing of a family. We ought not to be shocked by the curse of rags to riches and back again in just three generations. It is a law of nature.

'In fact, we should be utterly stunned and amazed when a family is able to navigate business and wealth *and* stay connected as a family.

'Does that make sense?' enquired the advisor.

'Yes, 100 per cent. We can see that money is already causing issues in the family, and it's just adding to the pressure we feel to find a solution,' said John. 'So are you going to tell us the solution now or what?'

The advisor smiled and responded, 'Of course. But that's tomorrow's adventure. Go away and think about what we've covered today. As well as all the challenges that come from the way our brain develops from "not ready" to "ready", there is also a profound misunderstanding about happiness.

'Contrary to popular opinion, money can't buy happiness. The opposite is often true because the presence of money, especially within a wealthy family, can actively work against happiness because those who grow up with money don't have to worry about finding a way to make a living and create competence in their lives, they don't therefore create autonomy, often getting an allowance all through life and they are never sure whether they have friends or people who are seeking favours. Science has shown very clearly that we need competence, autonomy and relatedness to be happy. In addition, money increases complexity and uncertainty – the twin enemies of happiness. By purposefully addressing their issues we can mitigate their negative impact.'

'Sounds great,' said Ayesha and John in unison.

'I'm famished, let's go and grab some dinner somewhere and we can chew this over as well!' added John.

Fourth (and Final) Meeting: The Solution

'Morning, great to see you both again,' opened the advisor. 'So today we are going to solve this Gordian Knot of a problem so you and your family can get on with enjoying your lives. I'm going to explain the process; there's a lot of work involved in implementing it, but at least you'll know it's possible.'

'Great – we are ready and we will gladly do the work,' chimed John.

'Absolutely!' agreed Ayesha. 'I'm just so excited to know there is a proven map we can follow to get us unstuck.'

'Fantastic – let's dive in … What you need to know is that managing love, loyalty and family wealth successfully generation after generation comes down to your willingness and determination to allow four distinct voices to be heard:

1. The business or balance sheet must have a voice (Strategic Plan).
2. The founder(s) must have a voice (Personal Plan(s)).
3. The individual family members must have a collective voice (Family Charter).
4. The family community must have a voice (Family Retreat).

'And governance is what facilitates the emergence of these crucial four voices. Governance is about answering the question, "How do we make decisions?" Remember, I said that the one thing every family business is always woefully short on is objectivity. The governance process I'm going to lay out is engineered objectivity. It is an agreed set of rules about how decisions will be made and how issues will be resolved, before those issues arise, that binds the family together.'

Pointing to the initial three-circle model on the whiteboard, the advisor created a new three-circle model ...

'Right ... now, the Jacksons' three circles of family, business and ownership (wealth) are virtually indistinguishable from each other ... Your goal is to separate those circles consciously and deliberately using governance and stewardship.'

'Sounds good,' said Ayesha. 'Is there a system to achieve this?'

'Yes, let me explain,' said the advisor. 'First, you need to separate the business circle. To begin the process of separating the business from the family and its ownership or wealth, Jackson Developments & Construction must be given a personality independent of the two of you as co-founders. Up to this point, you are the business. The name of the business is your name. You are also the walking, talking governance system of your business, as you are the decision-making protocol – engineered by you both, imposed in large part by John.'

John laughed and Ayesha rolled her eyes. They both knew that what the advisor was saying was true.

'So, I'm right about that then!' said the advisor. 'John, you make all the key decisions and everyone knows it. You may include Christopher, Nathan and Priya in the decision-making process along with key non-family staff, but you have the final say, and everyone is clear about that. And hey – that is totally understandable and probably works well.

'But, for the business to take on its own identity, it must be separated from *your* identity. This is achieved via the preparation of a strategic plan. The strategic plan speaks for the business. It is not the ambitions of the individuals in the business – in this case, you, Christopher, Nathan and Priya. It is the ambition of the business when it is fully realising its potential, understands the marketplace and delivers a meaningful, credible service or function within its community for profit. All the employed family members and key non-family employees are encouraged to contribute to that strategic plan, but the resulting agreed plan speaks only for the business. The true test is that the plan is the right plan in the hands of any collection of suitably qualified professionals. People's names do not appear anywhere in the plan.'

'Okay, but we have a strategic plan, we're not that backward!' said John, a little indignantly.

'I'm sure you do, but does your strategic plan go into enough detail to allow you to assess the agreed direction against the current capability in the business?' the advisor asked. John did not answer.

'Do you have a copy of the existing strategic plan that we could have a look at, John?' probed the advisor. 'I'm sure between us we can then answer that question.'

'Well, not really. It's not written down as such, but everyone knows what we are trying to achieve, including preferred markets, profitability and strengths that we play to,' said John.

'So am I right in thinking,' enquired the advisor, 'that the strategic plan lives in your head?'

'Well ... yes,' admitted John. 'But everyone knows what we are aiming for, and we do have a one-pager that outlines some key issues.'

'Okay, but it's not enough,' said the advisor. 'That said, this is a very common response. So I'm going to tell you what I've told countless founders before you: if your strategic plan is not written down, *you don't have* a strategic plan! If it is in your head, then I promise you, everyone doesn't know what you are collectively aiming for. For some founders I've met, they like the mystique of having the plan in their head so they can remain the driving genius in the business. For others, like yourself, I suspect it is just a timing issue. You probably have not considered it important enough to step back from the running of the business to document the corporate memory and plot a future course. Is that fair?' asked the advisor.

'Maybe,' conceded John.

'The thing is John,' added the advisor, 'even if you did have a brilliant strategic plan in your head, it would still be your voice coming through the strategic plan. What we need is for the business to have its own voice – separate from you and Ayesha.'

The advisor continued, 'Without a clear and rigorous strategy, it's really hard to determine whether you have the right people in the business to deliver on that strategy. Instead, you rely on filling gaps or moving people sideways to cover shortfalls or possibly trying to shoehorn family members into those gaps. But with the right strategic assessment, including employed family members and non-family members alike, you can finally answer the question, "Does the business currently have the experience, capability and skillset necessary to deliver on the strategy?" With a well-articulated strategy that considers the landscape inside and outside the business, it becomes possible to assess employed family members' relationships with the business.

'One of the reasons you are stuck is you are unsure if any of your children should or could take over the business. From what you've told me, they each have their own strengths and weaknesses, making that decision difficult. Is that right?'

'Yes – spot on,' said John. 'Christopher is the oldest and if he was more interested in the actual building side of things, rather than just the architecture and design, he would be the logical choice, especially as he is the oldest son. But I just don't think his heart is in it. Plus, he and Nathan don't get on. Priya is smart as a whip, but I'm still struggling to change my view that construction is not a suitable industry for a woman. I just don't want her having to deal with the sexist nonsense that happens on building sites.' John paused for a moment and realised the incredible irony in what he had just said, but continued anyway: 'Nathan is gung-ho and really enthusiastic, but he leads with his gut. He's not got the brains of the other two to step back and see the bigger picture. His decision making is too rash for the top job – certainly just now.'

'Okay, I totally understand that,' said the advisor. 'But there are two issues with that explanation. The first is that you are essentially looking at each of your children and assessing who you might be able to shoehorn into the position, rather than looking at the business to determine what *the business needs* to move forward. And secondly, you are relying on your own impression of each of them, which we have already established is clouded by your own family dynamics and default settings. You don't actually know!'

'That's very true,' said Ayesha. 'Are you saying we need to look at it from a different angle and work out what the business needs to meet its strategic objectives first and then establish who is best placed to take it there – and it may not even be one of the kids?'

'Yes, exactly, Ayesha,' confirmed the advisor. 'Without a detailed strategy, the business is revolving around your skills, knowledge and experience. It does not have a voice of its own. You talk of Nathan leading with his gut – does that remind you of anyone? To what extent is that the characteristic that has brought the business to this point? But you are right, it may not be what is needed to grow the business into the future. It's therefore essential to facilitate an objective measure of capabilities and match those against what is needed in the business now, as opposed to what was needed when you started the business. To deliver on the Jackson Developments & Construction strategy, does the business need the types of skills and experience that Christopher, Nathan and Priya have? Only when the strategic plan is clearly spelled out can that question be asked and answered, objectively rather than subjectively. If they don't have the needed skills, are they willing to train to get them? If they do have the needed skills, the next stage would be to define the commercial relationship between each family member who is employed in the business, and the business itself.

'I'm wondering, how do you currently pay Christopher, Nathan and Priya?' asked the advisor.

'They get a decent salary. Chris's architecture practice bills me the same amount as I pay Nathan, and Priya gets about $10,000 less, but they are potentially owners, so … '

'So … what?' enquired the advisor. 'Are you saying you pay them less than you would someone else doing a similar role because they are your children and will, presumably, inherit the business?'

'Well, yes, but there's more to it than that,' stressed John.

'You're not going to like this, John, but there is not more to it than that! There is no justification for paying your children less than they are worth as a cost-saving measure in lieu of future returns. Having this type of family subsidy and continuing it for as long as possible is a common mistake in family business. Senior leaders with the family surname are routinely underpaid based on the assumption that they are also owners and will eventually inherit the business. So what? Are you saying that Christopher, a qualified architect, Nathan, a hard worker who has worked his way up through the business, and Priya, a qualified engineer, should be happy to compromise their immediate real-world human value for some hypothetical future world value – just to subsidise Jackson Developments & Construction? Surely, you see that's nonsense – right? It's dangerous, and it has to stop at the first opportunity. As soon as any family business can afford to pay employed family members a commercial going-rate salary, the sooner that family can steer its way out of the murky waters of uneven or unfair distribution.

'And,' added the advisor, 'this professional commercialisation of the employment contract between employed family members and the business can now be done accurately because their activities form a part of the structure, which supports the strategy. The strategy is, in turn, endorsed by the shareholders, who fund it. In other words, having clear strategic objectives for the business allows each employed family member the opportunity to see if and how their current skillset fits into the strategic vision. And of course, it also gives you the same clarity.

'When the strategy is done, it will be independent of you or any other employed member of the Jackson family. It will be the independent voice of Jackson Developments & Construction, and that business will finally be able to establish an arrangement where the relationships with each family and non-family employees are based on their respective capabilities, skills, knowledge and proven performance – rather than their surname. Nothing else is relevant.

'This role clarity and definition is achieved through well-drafted position descriptions. The institution of job descriptions commercialises the relationship between family members and the business. Commercialising the relationship is done by answering the question, "What would it cost us to employ somebody new with this skillset?" There are two forces that need to be governed regarding the commercialisation of each position. First is the evidence test, which is, broadly, "What salary does a person with that experience typically command in this industry in this location?" And the second is the unique test, which is, "Does that individual have any special characteristics that would entitle them to a different compensation arrangement?" And, just to be clear, having "Jackson" as a surname is not a special characteristic. But Christopher having a separate business with access to a larger team of architects and design professionals might be.

'Once the strategic plan and performance contracts are complete, Jackson Developments & Construction has its own voice, separate from you. It is articulated by the collectively agreed strategic plan. Any family members in the business are now in a role that is needed to achieve that strategic plan, and they are in that role not because they are family members but because they have already demonstrated the capability, experience and skillset to deliver their part towards that strategic objective – or they have used that clarity to make a different choice.

'Do you see the value of this first voice via the strategic plan?' asked the advisor.

'I think so,' said John. 'In effect, you are saying that I no longer need to make the choice that has been keeping me up at night. Instead, by engaging our family and key employees in the creation of a strategic plan that everyone agrees with, endorses and is excited about, that direction is what will help to determine where each of them fit into the business, or not, depending on what the business needs and whether they want to be in a particular role.'

'Yes, exactly,' said the advisor. 'In a sense, it is no longer your decision. It's the business's decision based on a shared vision of where the business is heading.'

FOURTH (AND FINAL) MEETING: THE SOLUTION

'That sounds amazing,' said Ayesha. 'And I can't really see how anyone could even argue about that!'

'It certainly makes it easier,' added the advisor. 'Can I ask, how do your children feel right now?'

'I think above all else they are confused and frustrated at the status quo,' said Ayesha. 'Especially Priya. She knows John doesn't believe construction is a suitable profession for a woman. He's never said it, of course, but he doesn't need to. I think Christopher feels guilty and is trying to make everyone happy, and Nathan is irritated because he thinks he's "doing all the work".'

'Exactly,' said the advisor. 'They don't know what's possible or what they want, so they are in this weird limbo waiting for you to make a decision. It may very well be that a great deal of your confusion and frustration will disappear when their confusion and frustration disappear. The strategic plan is the first part of that puzzle, and the personal plans are the second. I'll explain that in more detail in a moment, but in short, the personal plans allow everyone in the business to engage with their own capabilities and aspirations. That process may illuminate for Priya that she doesn't want to be in the business, for example, and you have one less problem. But, if your children do decide to stay in the business, there must be a genuine role for them – one that supports the strategy and one where they are paid the going market rate for their respective positions. That salary must not be altered in any way (up or down) because of their familial connection to you.

'This disregard of familial relationships to position or compensation puts your children on a solid commercial and professional footing that then separates the business circle from the family and ownership or wealth circles. Christopher, Priya and Nathan may still be employed by the family business, but if they are, they are treated the same as any other key non-family employee. Their surname becomes irrelevant in the context of the business and working towards the strategic objective. This allows each sibling, including Anika, who is not employed in the business, to arrive at the beneficiary or ownership table as an equal. Plus, Nathan can't claim that Christopher is making more because his business is billing Jackson Developments & Construction, and Christopher and Priya can't be irritated because their qualifications aren't being recognised or compensated for. By taking these crucial governance steps, you put an end to any real or perceived family subsidising and ensure the right person is in the right role to deliver on the agreed strategy. It's no longer a decision you need to make. It's a decision that will be made because capabilities required to reach the strategic objective are matched to existing capabilities or a willingness to train to secure those capabilities.

'And, perhaps more importantly, the Jackson business circle has been successfully separated from the family circle and the ownership circle. Does that make sense?'

Both John and Ayesha nodded. Finally, there seemed to be a glimmer of hope that all was not lost and that something might be able to be done to help the business and the family.

'Okay,' continued the advisor. 'Now we need to separate the family circle. To do that you need to understand what the family wants. What are Christopher's personal dreams and aspirations? Do you know what Priya really wants to achieve in life? Do you have any idea what Nathan is aiming for? And what about Anika? Do you know what your children want? Forget the business for a moment — as individual human beings, what do your children dream of?'

'I don't know, we don't talk about that sort of stuff,' said John. 'I know Anika wants to create a successful restaurant, but beyond that I have no idea!'

'Don't feel bad about it,' said the advisor. 'Most people haven't got a clue. The solution is a personal plan. These personal plans ensure that each family member, regardless of whether they are currently employed in the business or not, is given a voice. They are charged with the responsibility of clearly and openly declaring the future they want for themselves. It's worth pointing out that personal plans are not compulsory – until a family has a business or shared wealth. Even then, it is okay for an individual to step away from the business, family or wealth and divine a private pathway. However, if that individual is to govern their wealth, and if family members intend to influence that wealth, they must declare their hand; otherwise, the family is governed by default settings. The resulting plans, which cover personal and professional aspirations, describe what success looks like for each member of the family over a set period. Too often, these questions are left unasked and unanswered, so no one knows what the others want. Personal plans bring those aspirations out into the open so that you can say, as parents, founders and life partners, "This is our plan for our future. It provides a clear basis for understanding what drives our point of view about both the business circle and the ownership circle." Your children no longer need to wonder; instead, they can figure out if they want to fit into that picture via the business or not. They can then make their aspiration clear to you. You can then guide and support your children on how best to make those aspirations a reality within the strategic direction of the business, or outside the business. Remember, this knowledge of aspirations led to your support of Anika. But that only happened because Anika was clear about what she wanted. Personal plans give that opportunity to your other children, too.

'Once that work is completed, everyone can sit at the table – business or kitchen – with the personality differences between each family member moderated. There is always a louder voice in every family. Sometimes that louder voice might come from the oldest or most domineering child, who is then the most likely to win an argument simply because everyone else gives up, or others don't have the ability to put their case forward with clarity. In your family, who has the loudest voice?'

'Oh, that's easy!' laughed Ayesha. 'John. If John isn't there, Nathan. The oldest, Christopher, has always struggled to get his point across without Nathan undermining him or making fun of him. The girls can and do stand up for themselves, but they tend to pick their battles.'

'Makes sense,' said the advisor. 'The great thing about personal plans is they help nullify these typical family dysfunctions by giving each individual family member a voice while also helping them to gain clarity about what they want in their own future, either inside or outside the business. Never underestimate the influence you both have had on the career choices and life paths of your children. The name of the business is Jackson Developments & Construction. Every conversation at the dinner table for the first 20 or so years of their lives involved Jackson Developments & Construction. Every Saturday job was at Jackson Developments & Construction. Whether deliberate or not, you have influenced the path or perceived career path for your family. Personal planning presses the pause button on that influence and encourages each of your children to really consider all their options. What is it they *really want*? This clarity allows each family member to step into their own journey with authenticity and ensure that they get to the negotiating table equally. This isn't about equal weight of each voice in relation to the business; however, should your voice have any more influence on the lives of your adult children than their own? Only you can decide your shared future. And the same is true for Christopher, Priya, Nathan and Anika, along with their partners.

'This process also creates a rational and logical opportunity to include their partners. Again, the mistake that is frequently made in family businesses is that it's just too complicated to involve the second generation's partners. It's not. Each of your children has one vote. If they are in a relationship, they still have one vote, only now that single vote is shared with their partner 50/50. That partner's voice is therefore heard in the preparation of the personal ambition of each of your children.

'For example, when Christopher prepares his personal plan, he will do so with his wife Rya. They might talk about where they want to live, where they want their children to grow up, what schools they want their children to go to and what opportunities they want their children to have, what career path Christopher wants for himself and what career path Rya wants. These are likely to be issues they have already discussed, and all of them can be accounted for and taken into consideration when thinking about the future pathways for them both. The same is true for each sibling. Their plan will include their partner, and their partner will have shared influence regarding anything that impacts their unique family.

'Once this is complete, all four children are well represented. Instead of waiting and wondering if or how they might fit into the family business at some point in the future, they step back and assess what *they really want to achieve individually*. Those aspirations may or may not involve the business, and they may or may not be possible, but at least they are each setting the agenda. They have stepped out of the shadow of the business, if only for an afternoon, to genuinely consider their own future and what they want that future to entail. That clarity can be liberating and energising for your children and you as the founders of the business.

'Each family member has their own voice irrespective of their role in the business, and their partner's voice is represented in that plan. And each of your children knows what they want to achieve in the years ahead and has a plan to deliver that outcome.

'It's important to reiterate at this point that the personal plans are *personal*. They are used to empower the planner, the individual. In this case, you both own your plan, and your children own their own plans. And when each person presents their personal plans to the family, they do not share the information verbatim. They don't include any judgements or comments they have made about other family members. This means that, instead of hearing, "This is what I think of you" the family hears, "This is what is important to me, what I want to achieve, and how I intend to go about it."

'The next step in the process to separate the family from the business and wealth is to create a structure around the way Jackson Developments & Construction makes decisions moving forward. John, you've said you want to step back, but you're worried that if you do, Christopher and Nathan will just argue endlessly. The personal planning process will allow you to see a way forward for the first time. The information from these personal plans allows you to be cognisant of everybody's individual points of view which, in turn, allows you to move away from the founder role to a stewardship role. As steward, your role is to help the family define a destination that everyone can get behind, which will take the whole family on the journey together where each family member feels valued. The direction of travel and making sure the family stays intact during that journey is much more important than the eventual destination. Stewardship therefore begins with individual wellbeing; transitions into team effectiveness; and ultimately leads to larger family business considerations such as ensuring that family values and missions remain relevant and contemporary.'

The advisor continued: 'John, if you, as the current walking, talking governance framework, are to step back effectively and with confidence, a replacement governance framework needs to be installed so that everyone in the business, family member or non-family member, knows how decisions are made: by whom, when and in what forums. What belongs at the dinner table, what belongs at the board table and so on. These decisions may include aspects such as how to endorse the business strategy, who to appoint to hold board seats, and what to do with the shared family assets. These and countless other decisions will be documented in a Family Charter. The Family Charter also affords the whole family an opportunity to create a culturally complete set of family values that are agreed and implemented as an institution through the family and the business, that will live on through the charter to inspire generations to come.'

'So, hang on, the Family Charter is different from the personal plans?' asked Ayesha.

'Yes,' said the advisor. 'Think of the strategic plan as giving the business a voice, the personal plans as giving each individual family member a voice, and the Family Charter as giving the family a voice. All are necessary to separate the circles. A Family Charter needs to be authored to document values and how the family makes decisions. This will include how the Jacksons make decisions about personal assets and the expectations your children may place on those assets while you are both alive and after you're gone. Sorry to be so blunt. For example, I understand you own a ski lodge. Do you have any expectations or hopes around that asset?'

'Well, yes actually,' said John. 'We have always had such great family holidays there, so we would like that property to be the place the family comes together at least once a year to ski and enjoy each other's company – no shop talk.'

'Okay, well, that would go in the charter. You are not saying the family must do that after you die, but right now, as the asset exists, you would like this wish to be known to the family. Without this knowledge and its formal expression, the question "what should we do with the lodge?" can become a trigger for default settings.

'The charter should also set out how the family makes decisions about endorsement of the trading business's strategy, and about the career pathways or migration of non-employed family members into the business or into and out of positions of influence. Remember, I raised the question of what might happen if you decided to bring Anika into the business to manage the family assets. This is a great example, the Family Charter would specify what Anika or anyone else up for that role would need to do in order to qualify for the position. This may include certain qualifications and a certain number of years of experience before qualifying for that role. This sort of detail prevents the wrong people from being slotted into the wrong roles just because their surname is or used to be Jackson.

'And the Family Council is the body that governs the charter and ensures it is up-to-date and remains relevant. A Family Council includes representation of all generations that have reached the age of majority.

'If the business is being discussed, the Family Charter or the Family Council decides whether to invite non-family employed representatives into the meeting to advocate or speak for the business so that a family member's position is not compromised. This ensures family members are not expected to wear two hats at once. The role of the CEO of the business may be laid out together with performance expectations of that role and what will happen if that person decides to step down or doesn't meet the required standards. The Family Charter is a comprehensive document that covers a vast range of possible future scenarios and how they will be dealt with and decided upon. And the Family Charter is created and agreed collectively, and reviewed periodically. This document is crucial in the separation of the family circle from the business and ownership circles.'

The advisor continued: 'In addition, family matters must be systematically removed from the business. Every family business starts life in a place where the family, the business and the wealth are indistinguishable from each other – we talked about that right at the start. This marks the start of a journey. Once the business is a large, successful business like yours, you need to purposefully separate the family, the business and the wealth (the three circles), which is paramount. The irony is that they will be separated eventually anyway – only they will be ripped apart when catastrophe strikes, such as your death, John, or ill health. The removal of family affairs from the business is part of the process and represents a shift to mature and disciplined administration of family affairs.

'Typically, this is known as a "family office", but this is a terrible term. The idea of a family office causes nothing but grief because it

FOURTH (AND FINAL) MEETING: THE SOLUTION

triggers a whole bunch of default settings about bureaucracy, as well as waves of intense emotional reaction from anger through to stonewalling. While the term is dangerous and unproductive, the idea is not.

'Do you find that you are asking people in your business to do things that are related to the family?' asked the advisor.

'I try not to, but it's impossible to avoid at times,' admitted John.

The advisor continued: 'Looking at your balance sheet and recognising the size of the business I can assure you that the time has now passed where it is appropriate to ask a member of staff if they could pick up your grandchildren from school, and it probably feels bizarre to be asking a PA to organise travel arrangements for the family to your Hamilton Island holiday home, while also organising John's birthday bash. As Jackson Developments & Construction has grown and employed more and more people across different locations, the family's personal or non-business affairs have almost certainly become a burden on the business. It's time for the two to be separated. How that's done will depend on you and how you choose to answer the question, "What is a better or different way to manage the family's personal, non-business affairs?"

'Those personal and non-business affairs might be investment advice for the children, or how to manage the family's recreational assets and provide equitable access to them. It might include organising the family rhythm or meeting agenda, the calendar of family events, the funding, booking or organisation of family events, as well as travel, managing frequent flyer points, or the funding and investment in education for your children and future generations.

'My guess is that you have certainly reached the point where your personal affairs are more than an executive assistant can or is willing to handle, and it's time for change. Even the use of a EA for personal matters is increasingly frowned on.'

'Yes, I am aware of that, and I'm conscious we need a different solution,' admitted John.

'The tipping point where separation becomes essential is that moment where your family's affairs, personal and non-business, are of a magnitude or dimension that, to continue to have the business manage them, causes many negative outcomes.

'There are several practical and financial considerations that make the separate management of personal matters effective. First, employed members of the business must no longer be asked to do things that are prone to misunderstanding, appear demeaning or worse, appear to be seen by others as a means of "infiltrating the family". Your staff must not be put in awkward situations that have no bearing on their job description. The other benefit is that this entity, whatever it is called, now contains most of your joint personal assets that have no bearing on or relevance to the business. It will include the holiday home and the ski lodge, as well as any other properties or assets you have. Before resisting this careful rearrangement of assets due to potential costs (tax and duties), a genuine cost/benefit analysis should be undertaken. Creating such an entity, therefore, shifts the dynamic between you and your children as their relationship with the family's shared wealth is through this entity rather than through you personally. Your grandchildren might request a small stipend to assist them through university, for example, but that request, outlined and agreed as possible in the Family Charter, would be made to this entity – not to you directly as "granny and grandad". And whatever arrangement is agreed in the Family Charter would be available to all your grandchildren equally should they seek assistance through university.

'Once the work on the Family Charter is complete, the business and family circles are largely separated. The business has a voice and the family has a voice. Can you see how this process will make your life so much easier, minimise disputes and allow you to know the business is in safe hands and the family is still connected and happy?'

'Absolutely,' said Ayesha. 'This seems like a formula for sustainability, allowing our wealth to be a catalyst for family togetherness, rather than a wedge.'

'Okay, fantastic,' said the advisor. 'Now there's just one more circle to disentangle from the current family arrangements and business: the wealth.

'Clearly, Jackson Developments & Construction has been extremely successful and the business has created significant wealth. That wealth should be governed by shares, titles, trusts and registered interests. As such, at least in theory, it is the easiest to define. The relationship between the family and the wealth should be outlined in the Family Charter. Beyond that, do you hope to pass both the wealth and potentially the business on to your children in some form or another?'

'Well, yes, of course,' replied John and Ayesha in unison.

'Again, the rules and decision-making protocols regarding the wealth will be spelt out in the Family Charter.

'For the record, when we talk about love, loyalty and wealth, we are not talking about the compulsory inclusion of a trading business. In your case, there is a transition of wealth and a trading business, which is the most complex. But if you have friends who have a balance sheet without a trading business, that still needs to be managed. You may appoint investment advisors to ensure the family wealth is governed properly, but there is less complexity. That said, a balance sheet still needs a similar governance framework, individuals being able to speak for themselves together with clear decision-making rules around the balance sheet.

'The last piece of governance is around philanthropy. Like many other families with wealth, you are likely to want to use at least some of that wealth for the greater good. This adds even more complexity and uncertainty about whether your gifting is well placed. I know you are especially concerned about this, Ayesha. You're not sure if your gifting is achieving what you intend. Most jurisdictions provide legal instruments to facilitate philanthropic governance. In Australia, it's called a private ancillary fund (PAF), and it has useful tax incentives. There are lots of rules around the use of PAFs, but they are well governed. What's especially useful about PAFs is that they can only invest in things that are properly endorsed and evidenced to be community-focused. They can't be used as a family slush fund. The institution of a Jackson PAF might be useful to aid in the separation of the circles.

'It's also worth noting that, whether you like it or not, you've created sustainable wealth. This means that there are problems brewing that subsequent generations will face if you don't face them now. How to manage wealth and how to best navigate the legislative frameworks around wealth will almost certainly change. The world is changing, the divide between rich and poor is widening, and there will be a reckoning. There must be. Add a Covid-19 global economic slump, and the cries for high wealth taxation and greater equality are inevitable. A changed regulatory environment that puts limits on how much wealth an individual can retain and control is not out of the question. Ensuring future generations are equipped to deal with these changes and actively engage in philanthropy to use that wealth for the greater good is therefore important.

'Once this work has been done, you will have a full and comprehensive governance framework. You will no longer be stuck,' added the advisor. 'The circles will have been purposefully and respectfully separated and a great deal of the complexity and uncertainty will have been removed from the family and the business.'

'Great!' said Ayesha. 'So how do we start?'

'Well, we might begin by letting the appropriately qualified professionals provide the right advice on the ownership circle. What is owned? How is it owned? And how does it transition to the next generation under the auspices of the state law, trust law or contract law? Then you have the business circle. It's now governed under the auspices of the strategic plan. The strategy defines the structure, and the structure then defines the possible employment paths that Christopher, Priya and Nathan can pursue based on properly specified roles that have meaning and value. Should Anika ever want to join the family business, the same process will apply, and she will only be given a job that is required to deliver on the strategic plan and that she is qualified for.

'Later, should any of the family members leave the business and want to rejoin, the same process will apply, and they will only be given a job that is required to deliver on the strategic plan and that they are qualified for or are willing to become qualified for.

'Each family member must then demonstrate their capabilities and subject themselves to the same rigour and discipline as any other employed person in the business, including annual reviews, skills assessments and appropriate training and development.

'As a result, when all four siblings are sitting with you enjoying a family dinner, Anika – who is not paid a salary because she doesn't work in the business – no longer has to worry whether she has the right to access the family ski lodge or holiday home. There is no inference, real or perceived, that she is at the back of the queue because she is not employed by the business. Why? Because the family, business and ownership or wealth circles have been separated through governance. The only debate is who wants to visit the lodge and when. If Priya and Nathan would like to visit in the same week, then the family applies the tie break that appears in the Family Charter. Anika can expect the same as her siblings who are employed in a business in terms of distribution of wealth or access to family assets. And should Christopher, Nathan or Priya want to borrow money from you in the same way Anika did for her restaurant, they can expect the same repayment terms. But all such decisions are clearly laid out in the Family Charter. Whether the siblings are employed by the business or not is irrelevant to distribution. Those who are employed are paid a proper commercial salary for their contribution and have equal rights to the ownership or wealth as those who have chosen to pursue a different path or career. If you are interested in equal distribution, then you'll consider all siblings equally, regardless of their relationship with the family business. No one will be worried about whether it was fair or not because the employed siblings are already compensated for their work via a going-rate salary, and all siblings will benefit from shareholder dividends, whether they are employed or not.

'The only touchpoint between the family as a family and the business is the family's right and obligation as shareholder influencers to endorse the strategic plan of the business, or to provide family constraints to the trading business. For example, the trading business might have restrictions on investment or trading with industries that the family believes are unethical or unsustainable. Everything else is left to the business and its management and leadership which, where that involves family members, is outlined in the Family Charter.

'At the family table, you will now have a governance framework driven by everyone being able to properly represent themselves. You will both be properly representing your ambitions for succession. And your children will be properly representing their ambitions for their future. They are each then able to sit at the table and engage in the Family Charter conversation and properly represent their views at the charter table. And through that process, you'll also have dealt fairly and equitably with your children's life partners because each partner has 50 per cent of their family's one vote; however, that is represented at the table.

'If you action this plan as steward, John, you will have successfully put your family in a position where you can all say:

- "We're well governed."
- "We're connected as a family."
- "We're not defined by our wealth, but we manage our wealth efficiently."

- "We're confident the business, our wealth and the family will endure for generations to come."
- "Each of us understands and respects our relationship with both the business and the wealth.'"

'I must say,' said John, 'I feel quite overwhelmed. I just couldn't see a way out of this without causing even more problems in the family. But you have walked us through a process, and from what you've told us, this is tried and well tested. Up to this point, I thought two things: firstly, that I would have to solve this problem (I guess that's my MO) and secondly, that I would have to invent the solution somehow. I really thought it would be a combination of good lawyers and good luck. It appears I don't need either! What you are demonstrating is that, like building a block of apartments, there is one best way to do this, and it works, and it is sustainable.'

'Yes!' confirmed the advisor. 'Collectively, this is the solution. It is always the solution. It is the solution for your construction company, and it is the same solution regardless of what the business does. And it can eradicate most of the complexity, uncertainty, as well as any lingering hostility or dysfunction that is so often viewed as inevitable in a family business. And it can ensure the continuation of love, loyalty and wealth. All you need to decide is whether you are ready to do the work.

'By purposefully ensuring that the business has a voice (strategic plan), you determine what the business needs to move forward and separate the business from you both as founders. When you also give each of your children a voice to determine what they really want and what they are capable of just now or are willing to learn in the future, you are no longer making a decision about succession; you are matching the needs of the business with the current and future capabilities of your children. All the while separating the business from the wealth so that if any of your children do decide to work in the business or are willing to do the extra training to be worthy of a position, then they are paid a going-rate salary for their work rather than a diluted salary on the basis that they may someday inherit the business. When the family also has a voice via the agreed Family Charter, then everyone understands the rules around the wealth of the business and how their own family can access that wealth in the future – whether they work in the family business or not. This is essentially the difference between being an employee and a shareholder or just a shareholder. We understand this distinction in a non-family business, but it gets lost in a family business. And finally, when the family community also has a voice via the Family Retreat, most of the uncertainty and complexity fall away.

'Governance calls on us to bring our neocortex to the table. Better-quality thinking means fewer default settings and reflex responses are triggered. The more governance, the less complexity and uncertainty, which provides the opportunity for ongoing family connectedness, harmony and happiness.

'The way we untangle this mess of neurological and biological human weaknesses is to understand and apply governance and stewardship. This allows you to remove the primary catalyst for angst. In addition, governance ensures that the business has a clear vision, and all employed family members are in roles they are suited to and paid properly for their contribution. The same goes for all non-family executives. All family members, regardless of role in the business, are shareholders and benefit accordingly through dividends and equitable access to shared assets. All family members are therefore able to sit equally at the ownership or wealth table regardless of whether they work in the business or not. No one is sidelined, and everyone is making and pursuing their own life goals, which may or may not be connected to the business. And perhaps more importantly, governance liberates the family and the business so that everyone and the wealth can thrive in a loving, connected family.

'To paraphrase author Michael Singer, "It's truly a great cosmic paradox that one of the best teachers in all of life, turns out to be death … Someone who has died could immediately remind you of the insignificance of the things that you cling to or teach you that men and women of all races are equal and that there is no difference between the rich and the poor because death instantly makes us all the same."'[15]

'I'm thrilled you have both decided not to wait for death to teach you that. When the four voices are heard, enduring success – bound by blood, underpinned by wealth and lived in harmony – is not only possible, but inevitable.'

'Amazing!' said John and Ayesha together, as John reached for Ayesha's hand. 'I honestly wasn't sure there was a solution, and I feel a little choked up that there is one and it's not impossible. Instead, there are just a few things we need to do and we will be on the right road.'

'I'm the same, John,' added Ayesha. 'It's such a relief – let's do it!'

Epilogue

Needless to say, John and Ayesha agreed that the work was necessary and invaluable. But they needed to get their children to agree. All four children were asked to read *Four Voices* and could also see the value in a more structured governance process that would help to eradicate the confusion and frustration that they were feeling.

Together they worked through the four voices so that:

1. The business (or balance sheet) has a voice.
2. The individuals (founder and family members) have an individual voice.
3. The family has a collective voice.
4. The family community (spouses and generations that follow) has a voice.

Priya took over as CEO under the mentorship of John. Nathan took over as Operations Director, also under the mentorship of John. The personal plans of both siblings allowed them to not only articulate what they wanted, but also a comprehensive skills audit helped to crystallise what was needed in each role and who had those skills or wanted to train to acquire them. Nathan came to realise that the intricacies of the CEO role were not for him and that actually Priya was better suited to that role. Priya was also willing to train further to strengthen her abilities in her new role. Nathan acknowledged that he was much happier and much more productive on-site, in his shorts and work boots. He started to really appreciate the dynamic that developed between him and Priya as CEO. He also started to enjoy seeing people underestimate her as CEO of a construction company.

Christopher came to embrace his love of architecture and instead stepped away from the business. The business instead entered into a service agreement with his company, and that business became a diversified asset of the parent company (Jackson Developments & Construction), with Christopher staying CEO of that business. The business also sponsored a strategic plan for Anika's restaurant, and it too became a shared family asset and part of the business's diversified assets. The family board would meet quarterly, where Priya and Nathan would update everyone on the progress of Jackson Developments & Construction, Christopher would report to the family on the progress of Jackson Architecture, and Anika would report on the progress of her restaurant, The Surf Shack. The Family Council would meet annually, and the whole family, including spouses and children, would get together for the Family Retreat.

Most of the angst in the business has disappeared. There are clear parameters of roles and expectations, and a clear outline of what happens if those expectations are not met. Each of the three businesses is growing, and each of the siblings is happy and connected. John is still involved in the business but has relished his role as mentor to both Priya and Nathan and enjoys hanging out with Christopher in his studio to get a better understanding of that side of the business – just because he wants to. For Christopher, this is a revelation, and he feels he can finally be himself without judgement. John's even been known to help in the kitchen at The Surf Shack. Ayesha is thrilled with the outcome. Not only does she get to spend more time with John, but he is far less stressed, and knowing her children are doing what they love in a supportive environment is all she's ever wanted.

Memories from the Family Retreat

SUNSET

AT THE WHITEBOARD AGAIN!

THE LAST DINNER

Endnotes

1. Hebb D (1949). *The Organization of Behavior*. John Wiley & Sons, New York.
2. Maté G and Maté D (2022). *The Myth of Normal: Trauma, Illness & Healing in a Toxic Culture*. Penguin Random House, London.
3. Nicholson N (1998). 'How Hardwired Is Human Behavior?' *Harvard Business Review*. hbr.org/1998/07/how-hardwired-is-human-behavior
4. Dawkins R (1976). *The Selfish Gene*. Oxford University Press, Oxford.
5. Nicholson N (1998). Op. cit.
6. Egan K (2008). *The Future of Education: Reimagining our schools from the ground up*. Yale University Press, New Haven and London.
7. Nicholson N (1998). Op. cit.
8. Dispenza J (2007). Op. cit.
9. Garfinkel H (1967). *Studies in Ethnomethodology*. Blackwell Publishers, Malden.
10. Csikszentmihalyi M (1990). *Flow: The classic work on how to achieve happiness*. Rider, New York.
11. Pink D (2009). *Drive: The surprising truth about what motivates us*. Penguin, New York.
12. Vonnegut K (1992). *Mother Night*. Vintage Classics.

13 Leman K (2009). *The Birth Order Book: Why You Are the Way You Are*. Revell, Grand Rapids, MI.
14 Jaffe DT (2010). *Stewardship in Your Family Enterprise: Developing Responsible Family Leadership Across Generations*. Pioneer Imprints.
15 Singer MA (2007). *The Untethered Soul: The Journey Beyond Yourself*. New Harbinger Publications, Oakland, CA.